DIVINE SPARKS

Interfaith Wisdom for a Postmodern World

By Starr Regan DiCiurcio

Cover design by Mark Hobbs.

Printed in the United States of America
Print ISBN: 978-1-953910-94-3
eBook ISBN: 978-1-953910-95-0

Library of Congress Control Number: 2021914159

Published by DartFrog Plus, the hybrid publishing imprint of DartFrog Books.

Publisher Information:
DartFrog Books
4697 Main Street
Manchester, VT 05255
www.DartFrogBooks.com

Join the discussion of this book on Bookclubz. Bookclubz is an online management tool for book clubs, available now for Android and iOS and via Bookclubz.com.

Names: DiCiurcio, Starr Regan, author.
Title: Divine sparks : interfaith wisdom for a postmodern world / by Starr Regan DiCiurcio.
Description: Manchester, VT : DartFrog Books, [2021]
Identifiers: ISBN: 978-1-953910-94-3 (paperback) | 978-1-953910-95-0 (Ebook) | LCCN: 2021914159
Subjects: LCSH: Self-realization. | Self-actualization (Psychology) | Meditation. | Mindfulness (Psychology) | Consciousness. | Identity (Psychology) | Values. | Wisdom. | Spiritual life. | LCGFT: Prayers. | Meditations.
Classification: LCC: BF637.S4 D53 2021 | DDC: 158.1--dc23

Advance Praise for *Divine Sparks*

Starr Regan DiCiurcio invites her readers to explore the inner land-scapes of their lives in wonder and reverence. She challenges every-one, of any religion or none, to make contemporary spiritual life directly relevant to our complex times. This insightful book is full of deep humanity, written with a wise heart and open mind.
—Rev. Diane Berke, Founder & Spiritual Director, One Spirit Learning Alliance

A beautiful lamp can be admired just sitting on a table, but once it is turned on its full colors shine. In the same manner, there is a Divine Spark in each of us and this book will help you turn on your own Divine Spark more fully. It will go deep within illuminating your spiritual quest as you shine ever more brightly. Wherever you are on your spiritual path— just now recognizing there is a path or a long-time traveler—this book will be a source to help your inner Divine Spark manifest brightly. Rev. Starr, a longtime journeyer, is the per-fect guide to open up new vistas for your exploration and this book provides a very specific map. Happy journey!
—Patricia Hunt Perry, Ph.D., retired Dharma Teacher, Plum Village Community of Engaged Buddhism

Starr Regan DiCiurcio has written a wise and heart-centered book that addresses issues central to our times. It is grounded in ancient truths and yet looks to the future by encouraging personal and soci-etal evolution toward a global ethic of love for all—all of humanity, the realms of flora and fauna and our precious planet.
—Mara Freeman, Druidess and author of *Kindling the Celtic Spirit* and *Grail Alchemy*

Each topic of *Divine Sparks* is a spiritual gem illuminating the heart on its path to inner peace and true happiness. Starr's writings enable us to savor and cultivate mindfulness and joy in our daily life. *Divine Sparks* is a treasured guide, leading us back again and again to the deep self, our home, where we may welcome all with love.
—Sr. Anne Leger, Co-director, Still Point Interfaith Retreat Center

Starr Regan DiCiurcio is the voice of wisdom in today's interconnected world. *Divine Sparks* is an indispensable resource and a treasure trove for clergy and faith communities, as well as a personal companion and guide across interfaith traditions. This book will enrich your perspectives, guide your interior spiritual journey, and inspire your life with hope.
—Rev. Ali Trowbridge, Pastor, Caldwell Presbyterian Church

Starr Regan DiCiurcio sparks the intrinsic spiritual potential of her readers across all faiths. *Divine Sparks* is an invitation to look deeply into the infinite source of possibilities as we search for what is good, true, and beautiful. This book will serve as an interfaith companion, the North Star on our Divine journey home.
—Sr. Mai Trang, Deer Park Monastery, Plum Village Community of Engaged Buddhism

With deep gratitude,
this book is dedicated to all the women and men
who have shared their spiritual lives with me,
and in memory of my anam cara, Pat Rambo.

CONTENTS

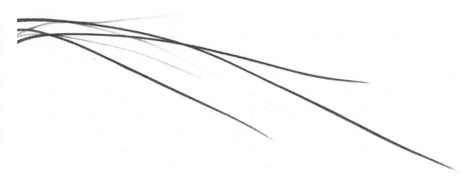

INTRODUCTION

"We live in the shelter of each other."
—Traditional Irish Saying

We all aim to be informed, aware, intelligent people. We spend much of our lives getting an education, training for jobs, and improving our knowledge base and skills. As we age, learning new things strengthens our brains and our sense of well-being. We have this natural inclination throughout our years to continue to grow. This attribute is unique to human beings, as far as we know.

This book is about spiritual awareness. It recognizes that this quest for understanding our world and our place in it reaches beyond intellectual pursuits. It is spiritual. Over the ages and in all cultures, we see a human hunger for connection to spirit. The idea of spirit is defined in many ways, but this experience of longing remains the same. It is part of who we are. For many, the search is just an occasional flicker, but for most of us, it is invariably present and acknowledged. For some, it is aflame. This spiritual longing manifests in a great variety of ways. It can be seen in formal, traditional prayers and rituals, or it can be encountered in connections with nature. Some people bridge into the spiritual realm through the arts, whether they are creators or devotees. Still others utilize pilgrimages and retreats as ways of nourishing their spiritual potential. And for us all, service is a potent portal to the Divine. What unifies all these experiences of sacred longing is a sense of wonder, the extraordinary encounter with mystery that can come into our daily lives.

In the postmodern era we are living in, there are unique and growing challenges. We move at increasing rates of speed. We are often distracted and not present to one another. Too frequently our conversations are shallow and perfunctory. Technology has brought significant tests to our brains along with its gifts. Life as we know it on this planet is dying. The world grows smaller, and we rub up against one another in ways that spark negativity, including intolerance and violence. Resources are becoming increasingly scarce, and we choose greed at least as often as generosity. Even in affluent countries, we are experiencing epidemics of depression, addiction, anxiety, and loneliness. Family and religious structures are crumbling and call for new forms of connection. The Chinese character for crisis is made up of two individual characters: danger and opportunity. This is a time of great opportunity. It calls for reflection, creativity, and activism. It calls us to tap into all our spiritual resources.

I am an interfaith minister. The term may be a new concept for you, as it is for many. This unique group of ministers manifests their work in varying forms. The training features counseling and all the usual ministerial roles, as well as exploration of the major wisdom traditions of the world. It includes learning how to create rituals for life's major transitions and practices for daily life that cross traditions and go beyond. Some people who train as interfaith ministers are already active clergy in various traditions. As I started seminary at One Spirit Learning Alliance, I was an ordained member of the Order of Interbeing (Tiep Hien Order) of Thich Nhất Hanh. My work has evolved to incorporate my Buddhist and Christian experiences, as well as my love of the arts. It is fed further by a deep connection to my Celtic ancestry. Another interfaith minister would have quite a different profile, but that is one of the strengths of this relatively new field of ministry. What unifies this work is an acknowledgment of the strong underlying source of wisdom that flows through all traditions and a commitment to loving, engaged compassion for all.

You are invited to join in an exploration of your own spiritual awareness as you read this book. It is a book designed for men and women of any faith tradition or none. In our times, there are countless people who have been wounded in their religious institutions of origin. This tragic reality calls us to form new ways of connecting spiritually. For every reader, I hope you'll find in these pages a plethora of ideas to enhance and grow your personal spiritual life.

This book is written in thirteen chapters that can be used by individuals or groups. You may wish to read it through quickly and then go back and work with it in a contemplative manner. The first twelve chapters can be read over the course of a year, taking one theme per month, or for those in a hurry, it could be read over twelve weeks.

The twelve themes selected were taken from the retreats I have led at Still Point Interfaith Retreat Center in New York State. All topics were popular with those who attended and enriching for me to prepare. If one of them seems especially critical to you right now, start there. The chapters may be read in any order.

You may wish to use this book with a group, alone, or both. The chapters each have an essay, questions for reflection, a creative stretch, and a concluding prayer or meditation. The thirteenth chapter is a collection of more of my prayers and meditations that can be used at any time. For group meetings, it would be preferable for everyone to read and work with each chapter before gathering. The discussions will be most beneficial after spending some time with the material individually.

This book is a companion. It can be returned to again and again as a source of refreshment, encouragement, and new ideas. Hopefully, it is a springboard for your own spiritual practice and will lead you to further heights of discovery.

All that I have to share I have been taught or led to through direct experience sourced in those teachings. My gratitude and love go to Gabriel Gomes, Jay Murnane, John O'Donohue, Thich Nhất Hanh, Patricia Hunt Perry, and Diane Berke. Equally important, my gratitude and love go to all the men and women I have worked with over the years in spiritual direction, retreat facilitation, meditation classes, hospice and mentoring for both One Spirit Seminary, and the Order of Interbeing. They have all been my teachers, and this book is dedicated to them.

To my family and friends, I bow and smile in acknowledgment of their understanding and support over the years. Included here are the amazing sisters of Still Point Interfaith Retreat Center. Sisters Rowena Fay (d. 2019), Anne Leger, and Nicole St. John have given me the opportunity to lead retreats for women at their center for over a decade. Their deep faith, delightful humor, and love-in-action have enriched my life and the lives of many others. To my dear friends, Mary Scanlan and Amy Thomas, who have taken the time to read my drafts and offer their suggestions, my great gratitude. At LARAC (Lower Adirondack Regional Arts Council), I was generously given a workspace for editing. Additional thanks go to Gordon McClellan, Ali Trowbridge, Katelynn Watkins, and all my new friends at DartFrog Books, whose professional skills have made this a better book. And as always, boundless gratitude and love to my husband Tom, who has been a patient draft reader, cheerleader, guiding light, and a source of unwavering strength. Although this work has my name on it, it is the fruit of the spirit of many. If you find any inaccuracies or disagreeable bits, those are mine.

With great love,
Starr

CHAPTER ONE

THE TRUE SELF

"My true self is free. I cannot be contained."
—Marcus Aurelius

What is the true self? There are many interpretations of the term, but for our purposes, let's think of it as the essential self, the part of us that is beyond all our roles and cultural shaping. It is this inner core that can get lost as we live our daily lives responding to the forces around us. These forces include our surrounding cultures of family, professions, peers, religion, race, nationality, and all the many features that form our outward identity. When we lose track of our true selves, we become unrooted, and suffering arises. It is our spiritual life that supports the true self and maintains its position of centrality in our days.

For many, the true self is also the place where God is reflected. It is here that we are open to the Divine Spark that is part of all life. It is the sacred center that is at the heart of all creation, in each and every being and in matter. The true self of each of us, of trees, water, rocks, and all that is, evokes reverence. Understanding this potential within us is key to living a life of spiritual grace.

In time, most of us come to define ourselves in terms of our life experiences. We are a mom or dad, a daughter or son, a doctor, bricklayer or teacher, a Christian or Muslim, an American or Italian, and on and on. Our identities are largely formed by the ways we move in the world. But we are more. We are much more.

Jack Kornfield teaches about an enormous Buddha statue in Thailand made of clay. The monks tending it noticed cracks and prepared to make the necessary repairs. While working, one of them found a gleam coming from deep within a dark crack. This led to the discovery of a Buddha of gold, outstanding among the statues of Buddha in Southeast Asia. It had been covered over in clay to protect it from discovery in times of unrest. Now throngs of pilgrims go to see the golden Buddha of Sukhothai.

We are like this Buddha. Covered in layers of clay, of protection, we are hiding our real strength and beauty. How can we become aware of our true selves, and how can we hang on to that awareness and its promise of peace and joy? Let's start at the beginning, before you were born.

BEFORE YOU WERE BORN

You were alive before the day of your birth, already created by the biological contributions of your parents. Their DNA formed yours, as their parents' had formed theirs. At conception, you became part of the web of life, going back through countless generations. In the religious traditions of the East and those of first peoples globally, there is a great deal of respect for ancestors. It is understood that we are a continuation of those who came before us. It behooves us to understand those ancestors and to know how we are a part of their evolving lineage.

In Thich Nhất Hanh's teachings, there are three categories of ancestors to consider: blood ancestors, spiritual ancestors, and land ancestors. Blood ancestors are your biological family; they are part of your life through your physical being. They also influence us through experience. For example, if you have a mother who was murdered, that trauma will not end with her but will be part of your life also. We all have these inheritances, negative and positive, to acknowledge and learn from. The second category, your spiritual ancestors, includes all the spiritual teachers that have had an impact on your life. Usually we meet these teachers starting early in our childhood, but not always. Third, we recognize the importance of our land ancestors, those who lived on the land before us. Wherever we are, we are living with the results of earlier generations. For better or worse, we are working with a rapidly changing environment. Mother Earth needs our responsible care more than ever, and the generations that come after us are counting on our determined reform.

So there are a number of forces already at play with our identity as we are born into a particular time and place, a particular family, a particular religion, or none at all. These forces continue to strengthen as we grow up, and soon we think we are our roles. For those raised in a religious community or with significant exposure to the natural world or the arts, there may have been some access to their true selves. But many were not that fortunate.

SPIRITUAL HISTORY

We cannot move forward if we are not at peace with our spiritual history. It is helpful to pause and reflect on how we have developed spiritually throughout our lives. There are important moments that have shaped who we are. It can simply be a list to start. Here is mine.

- Born into an Irish-American family, both Catholic and Protestant
- Summers spent on the St. Lawrence River in a great deal of solitude
- Dr. Gabriel Gomes explaining the Cosmic Christ in a college theology class
- Training as a yoga teacher and encountering the concept of "witness"
- Finding Thich Nhất Hanh's writing while teaching Vietnamese refugees
- Ordaining in the Order of Interbeing
- Becoming an interfaith minister
- Experiencing homecoming with John O'Donohue

This is a list of major events in my life of spirit. You will notice that these are all positive events. There would be a second list of challenges, equally important. My list would include a failed marriage that led me to seek spiritual direction through which I was introduced to the writings of Merton, Nouwen, and others. It would also include my struggles as a woman in the Roman Catholic Church. Fortunately for me, those places of pain have been well worked through in spiritual practice and with spiritual directors, so I have learned what I needed to learn and found peace.

Taking this type of inventory provides a baseline for exploration of an expanding, enriching spiritual life. After making your lists, you may wish to expound on any or all of your defining moments through writing, music, or artwork. You are invited to create your own history in the creative stretch section of this chapter. You may wish to further explore your experiences and all their implications in spiritual direction.

BEYOND EGO

As we reflect on our lives and all our ups and downs, we want to keep in mind why we do this exploration. It is not a self-indulgence, but rather a strengthening of self that can lead us to our higher selves. When we were children, we developed our egos in a way that made us able to move effectively in our daily lives. We need to have healthy egos in order to function, but as we mature, we benefit from moving beyond those egos, from self to Self. The small self is attached to the personal, to what benefits one's needs and wants. The large Self has moved beyond the immediate to a state of interconnection of all that is, through service and loving compassion. This eternal world beyond our small self is our goal in spiritual development. It is what Matthew speaks of in his gospel when he tells us that whosoever shall save his life will lose it. It is an invitation to you.

Any time we examine our lives, we should approach the process with curiosity rather than judgment. We stand outside ourselves and try to get an objective view. This is the position of witness taught by yogis that is so helpful. Judging, comparing minds are a trap and do not move us forward. My dharma teacher taught me that all comparisons are odious, and I have always tried to bring that to mind when I note them. So, what is helpful? Deep looking and deep listening are the practices to trust.

Deep listening is a skill to develop for your own sake and for the sake of all your relationships. In deep listening, we suspend our own commentary and listen to the speaker. We hear their words and see when they are finding it hard to speak. We notice what is not shared. This level of attention is not as easy as you might first expect. So often, we are running our own dialogue as someone else is talking. We are agreeing or disagreeing, arguing, thinking of examples, and most commonly, preparing our response! We are caught in our egos. It is a challenging practice to suspend all inner dialogue and simply be present to what is being said. One stays in the moment without bringing any history into the exchange. The goal is to be truly open. Then one can actually hear what is said, and when it is the right time, make a considered response. Often no response is needed. It is a gift to just be the listener for someone. Suspend advice, interruptions, or any comments unless they are invited. This gift of listening will deepen your understanding and compassion.

Deep looking asks much the same of us when we are observing an object or a set of circumstances. We are not bringing all our old stories to the situation. We are totally present in mindfulness, and we are non-judging. This opens us to see more clearly. In turn, that clarity provides access to a wider range of possible responses if needed. You can pause at any time and practice deep looking. If you are taking a walk, stop and look at something as simple as a flower or leaf. Truly look deeply, and you will be rewarded with a rich experience of life.

These practices of deep listening and deep looking are helpful as we try to understand ourselves and others. They make us less reactive and more considered in all we say and do. They broaden our minds and create more options for us. They help us make good decisions. As we grow in understanding, we grow in compassion. This is a linked process, and we can practice it daily. In this way, we come to understand our true selves and to know how to live our lives to the fullest.

ASPIRATIONS

As we come to more fully understand ourselves, we develop a set of values that we live by. These are often taught to us as children, but it is our life experience that refines and reinforces them. Since we are gifted with free will, we get to choose how we shape ourselves. The more reflective we are, the greater our degree of choice.

There is a Native American teaching story about two wolves that illuminates this point. An elder was instructing his grandchildren about life and told them of two wolves inside him who were having a horrible fight. One of the wolves represented all the negative energies, such as fear, anger, ignorance, arrogance, guilt, resentment, pride, and ego. The other wolf was the representative of love, joy, peace, compassion, generosity, truth, faith, and all things good. The grandfather explained to the little ones that the same fight goes on inside everyone. One of the children asked him which wolf would win the fight. The grandfather responded, "The one you feed."

What do you feed? What is important to you? What are your highest values, and what are your life's aspirations? An aspiration is something you can engage with right now. At this moment, you can decide the direction you wish to face and move toward. Aspirations are critically important to a life well-lived. Our aspirations are changeable and reflect the constant state of change in our lives. Because of this, we would be wise to frequently visit this question: what is my highest aspiration? The answer defines who you are.

DEALING WITH OBSTACLES

There are many obstacles that can interfere with our spiritual life. They pop up predictably and unexpectedly. They are brief, and they are relentlessly long. They are singular and manageable, and they are overwhelming. St. John of the Cross, a sixteenth-century mystic, struggled with "*the dark night of the soul.*" Mother Teresa shared her relentless trials in her letters to her spiritual directors. But no matter how challenging our obstacles are, there are some things we can do to learn from them and grow in spirit. Let's look at a few examples.

When you have people in your life who are not helpful, you have the opportunity to transform the relationship or how you view it. Often we can come to new understandings of ourselves, the person who troubles us, and contributing factors. Healing occurs. In other cases, relationships may need to be dismissed with finality. If there is lingering resentment, anger, or fear, we must be sure to heal these negative energies so we can come to wholeness and move on. Many times we need the support of others, friends or counselors, to do this.

There also can be certain environments, such as workplaces or places of recreation, that are not in alignment with our true selves. Sometimes making a change is very simple, but a change in these areas can be difficult. You may need a long-term strategy. How we spend our time is important and needs to be compatible with our highest aspirations. Carefully evaluate your work, your hobbies, and your leisure activities. See that they do not impinge on your integrity.

One of the most difficult areas to address is our habit energy. These are the deeply ingrained ways we move through our days without even thinking. Of course, habits can be very helpful if they are good ones. We don't want to have a debate with ourselves every morning about brushing our teeth. We simply do it. But when what we do, or think, or say is problematic, those habit energies need to be changed. All of us know how difficult this can be. Here is a formula to help you **REAP** the benefit of releasing bad habits.

- **R**ecognize what is happening. It is critical to become aware of the habit each time it manifests. At first, this may be all you can do. That's a solid first step. Just compassionately notice what you are doing. Smile to yourself and say, "Here I go again!"

- Evaluate your options. These might be short-term, multistep possibilities, or one direct route to change. What will work best for you? You may not know until you try, but that is part of making the change you wish to see.
- Apply the path you have chosen. How is it working? Does it need any tweaking? Can it be fine-tuned, or do you need to try a different option?
- Practice the new positive habit as much as needed. This step usually will last for quite a while, and you may experience many lapses. That is to be expected. If you persevere, you will **REAP** your rewards.

No matter what obstacles you face, know that you do not have to face them alone. Our human experience is shared, and you will find many others who are going through similar challenges. Your experience will grant you wisdom to help others, just as you benefit from those who encourage and teach you. Support groups are widely available, both formally and informally. Spiritual communities are a natural resource for us all, as are ministers, priests, spiritual directors, therapists, and other guides. Historical figures or contemporary teachers can offer their own experiences and resultant wisdom too. You can meditate, pray, and invite the companionship of angels, bodhisattvas, saints, and other great beings. As you try to work with any difficulty, be sure to take good care of yourself and, as much as possible, hold yourself lightly. As Julian of Norwich so wisely taught us, "*All shall be well, and all shall be well and all manner of thing shall be well.*"

FULLY ALIVE

"*True self is non-self, the awareness that the self is made only of non-self elements. There's no separation between self and other, and everything is interconnected. Once you are aware of that, you are no longer caught in the idea that you are a separate entity. It brings you insight. You know*

that your happiness and suffering depend on the happiness and suffering of others. That insight helps you not to do wrong things that will bring suffering to yourself and to other people. If you try to help your father to suffer less, you have a chance to suffer less. If you are able to help your son suffer less, then you, as a father, will suffer less. Thanks to the realization that there is no separate self, you realize that happiness and suffering are not individual matters. You see the nature of interconnectedness and you know that to protect yourself you have to protect the human beings around you."
—Thich Nhất Hanh

This teaching by Thich Nhất Hanh tells us why working toward a fuller understanding of our true selves is so important. Ultimately, it leads us to a deep, mystical connection to all of reality. We come to understand that we are not alone in life, but rather that we are intimately connected to one another, all beings, the earth, and the universe. It is this connection that underlies religious traditions and unites them. If we are to have the fullest of spiritual lives, it is this search for our place in the scheme of things that matters. Loving the search itself is a practice to embrace. Answers to our questions will come in time, or not. Answers are not the goal of spirituality, and a search for certainty is fruitless. It is our acceptance and celebration of the mystery of life we are privileged to be part of, that guides us and supports us. It is this connection to Mystery that ultimately brings us joy and freedom.

QUESTIONS FOR REFLECTION

The following questions cover a great deal of territory. Many include topics that are discussed in other chapters, but relate to your true self. Each one is an invitation to explore, now or later.

1. When were you happiest?
2. Who do you admire?
3. What is your relationship to your body?
4. What do you most value?
5. What do you still want to learn?
6. When do you feel most alive?
7. What is beautiful to you?
8. What are your greatest strengths?
9. How do you serve the world?
10. Do your thoughts, words, and actions align with your values?
11. How do you use your creative gifts?
12. What do you revere?
13. What lessons/gifts has suffering brought to you?
14. What is your highest aspiration?

CREATIVE STRETCH

1. Find or create images of your highest aspirations. Place them in locations where they can serve as reminders. When you stop noticing them, move them to new places or select new images.
2. Write your personal spiritual history. Start from childhood and bring it up to the present. It can be as simple as a list. Be honest. Leave nothing significant out. You may make one general list or two lists, one of perceived positive events and one of perceived negative events. This is for your own reflection. If you wish to share any of it later, you can choose how much, when, and with whom. You may expand this self-exploration through journaling, music, or the visual arts. But the list is the foundational exercise.
3. Choose an object to look at deeply. This may be a painting, a photograph, a flower, or anything you wish. Then let your mind release its thinking and just quietly observe. This is a time of being with, not of doing. Let your analytical mind go and rest in the experience. Do not strive for any particular outcome. Insight will come.
4. Find a partner and practice deep listening. Together, decide on a topic, a time limit, and who will go first. It is good to start with just a five-minute experience. The listener can use a bell, chime, or a simple word to signal when the speaker begins and ends. The speaker shares whatever is on his or her mind with care. The listener does not interrupt or speak in any manner, including expressions of face or body movements. The idea is to receive without judgment. If the listener talks or has physical reactions of surprise, anger, or any emotion, a conversation has started instead of deep listening. When the time is up, switch roles. If you wish, you can add comments or get clarification when the session is complete.

Prayer For My True Self

Banish all greed from my heart. Let me not be attached to sparkly things and seductive pulls.
Let me not cling to anything or anyone, and let me not be stingy.
Let me be generous in thought, word, and action. Let me give with an open hand.
May I move in this world with wisdom and love.
May I recognize and correct any falseness within.
May I be true to my Divine nature.

Let my anger be an alarm to injustice, a light on falsehood. But let me not act or speak in anger.
Let me be centered, patient, and kind. Let me be a peacemaker.
May I move in this world with wisdom and love.
May I recognize and correct any falseness within.
May I be true to my Divine nature.

Banish pride that leads me to selfishness and arrogance. Let not those forces of separation creep into my life.
Rather, keep me humble in my own eyes. Let me see I am only a speck of light in eternity.
May I move in this world with wisdom and love.
May I recognize and correct any falseness within.
May I be true to my Divine nature.

Let me not waste any day I am given. Let me treasure all the hours and the possibilities they offer.
And as I value needed rest, let me also value diligence and find joy in a productive and creative life.
May I move in this world with wisdom and love.
May I recognize and correct any falseness within.
May I be true to my Divine nature.

Let me not be cursed with excessive consumption in any form—sex, food, alcohol, drugs, or technology.
Let me guard my senses with care and open these gates only to what nourishes my total being.
Protect me from asceticism, addiction, and any compulsive inclinations.
May I live in balance, in mindfulness, and contentment.
May I move in this world with wisdom and love.
May I recognize and correct any falseness within.
May I be true to my Divine nature.

Banish any trace of envy from within me.
Open my heart to true joy for the good fortune of others. What enriches their lives enriches mine. We are one.
May I move in this world with wisdom and love.
May I recognize and correct any falseness within.
May I be true to my Divine nature.

Banish all ignorance remaining in me.
Fill me with a love of learning and let me continue to study and open myself to new teachings of intellect, intuition, and imagination always.
May I move in this world with wisdom and love.
May I recognize and correct any falseness within.
May I be true to my Divine nature.

Let my mind not reside in the false world of scarcity but rather recognize the truth of abundance.
Let my heart be filled with gratitude for all the beauty surrounding me.
May I move in this world with wisdom and love.
May I recognize and correct any falseness within.
May I be true to my Divine nature.

Let me not deceive myself or others with falsehoods.
Let me live with integrity holding high the truth as it is revealed to me.
May I move in this world with wisdom and love.
May I recognize and correct any falseness within.
May I be true to my Divine nature.

Banish all cowardice from my life. Fear is the great destroyer of love and has no home in my heart.
Rather let me be brave and understand that I walk not alone, but with brothers, sisters, and unseen angels.
May I move in this world with wisdom and love.
May I recognize and correct any falseness within.
May I be true to my Divine nature.

Release all disappointments, grudges, and hostilities I hold toward myself or others.
Give me their lessons, and then help me forgive and move on.
May I move in this world with wisdom and love.
May I recognize and correct any falseness within.
May I be true to my Divine nature.

Last of all, close not my heart. Let me understand that a closed heart is an unhappy heart.
Help me live a life of true hospitality, open to all that comes my way each day—each person, each challenge, each opportunity.
Let me come to understand that the direct path to joy and freedom is the path of service.
May I move in this world with wisdom and love.
May I recognize and correct any falseness within.
May I be true to my Divine nature.

CHAPTER TWO

MEDITATION AND MINDFULNESS

"Who looks outside, dreams; who looks inside, awakes."
—Carl Jung

T he practices of meditation and mindfulness have been utilized by many spiritual traditions across time. This is a testa-
ment to their proven effectiveness. It also offers promise as
a place where these traditions can come together to grow in understanding and appreciation for one another. We now can research
these long-established practices in ways that confirm what generations have experienced. Just some of the known benefits are the
lowering of blood pressure and heart rate, reduced stress and pain,
increased creativity, resilience, balance and awareness, improved
concentration, focus and memory, and better grounding with less
fear and anxiety. There are also a number of positive impacts on
the brain, including increased alpha rhythms and neuroplasticity,
thicker cortical walls, and synchronization of the left and right
hemispheres. Who doesn't want all this? If you are a regular meditator, you probably are aware of some resulting inner shifts that have
kept you returning to the practice. If you are new to mindfulness and
meditation, there is much to look forward to.

There are many ways to meditate. It is important to explore the
options until you identify what works best for you. In time, you may
find that what seemed perfect for a while no longer is, and it will be
refreshing to switch up your practice in some way. For some, these
are purely physical and mental exercises, but for our purposes,
meditation and mindfulness are spiritual experiences as well. The
spiritual dimension is entered when our practice is connected to
values, especially love, compassion, and wisdom. We do not strive

or try to achieve anything. Meditation is not goal oriented. It is an act of receptive awareness, open to all that is before us, listening and looking without judgment. This is a profound opportunity. It is important to enter your time of meditation with intention and a sense of preparation for the sacred.

THE FOUR MEDITATION POSTURES

In Eastern traditions, there are four classic meditation postures: sitting, walking, standing, and lying down. When you think of meditators, you probably bring to mind the image of someone sitting blissfully on a cushion or zafu. That is a fine choice if you are physically able. You may also use a kneeling bench or a chair just as effectively. The important thing is to be as physically comfortable as possible without nodding off into dreamland. You should feel grounded and stable in your seat. If you can, it is good to sit without leaning into the back of your chair. You may think of your energy flowing in two directions: first from your hips down, grounding into the earth, and second from your waist up, lifting to straighten your relaxed spine, creating a channel for your unobstructed breath. If you need to change your position during your meditation, do so slowly and mindfully. As you develop your practice, you may choose to sit with discomfort that arises, just noting it. We can sit for hours at the movies and not move a muscle, but when we meditate, all kinds of thoughts and feelings arise. Just notice them and release them. Of course, if you are in real pain, please pay attention to it and make any necessary adjustments.

Standing meditation is often done before a sacred image or outdoors connecting to nature's beauty. It is a posture of reverence in Buddhism, Judaism, and Christianity, especially Orthodox traditions. It is an important part of tai chi and Qi Gong. For many, it is deceptively difficult to stand for lengthy periods, but it is worth incorporating into your practice, perhaps standing before an altar and contemplating a sacred mystery or pausing in walking meditation for a few minutes. If doziness is a problem at any point during sitting meditation, standing is an effective way to handle it.

Walking meditation is practiced by bringing our attention to our steps and connecting to our breath. You may start by taking a step on your inhale and then another on your exhale. Experiment to see what provides you with a relaxed and aware experience of walking. Perhaps you will take one step on the inhale and three on the exhale. Follow your body's natural rhythms. It may be done at any rate of speed, but it is best to walk slowly while learning. With each deliberate step, you feel your connection to the earth and all its beings. You may wish to also employ a mantra as your walk, a simple word or phrase to help set your pace. The words may be connected to your breath, such as "in" and "out." Or you may wish to connect the words to your steps, such as "blessed" and "earth." Walk tall and look ahead. Try on a small smile. You can create this practice in a way that speaks from your heart and supports your intentions.

Your walking should be aimless, cultivating a sense of ease and peace. The Buddhist quality of aimlessness does not mean to lead an undirected life, but rather to live in the present without striving. If you have the opportunity, find a labyrinth to walk. Labyrinths help us cultivate aimlessness. The course is set; there is nothing to do but follow it. You may practice walking meditation anytime, anywhere. If you like, you may walk with a partner or a group. You may also invite someone deceased, or otherwise not physically present, to walk with you. Enjoy your time with them beside you, holding them in your heart. If you know others who are not able to walk, walk for them.

The last traditional meditation posture is lying down. Stretch out on your back, hands resting a few inches from your body with palms upward. It is good to keep your head in line with your spine, so if possible, use no pillow or a small one. Try placing a rolled-up towel or pillow under your knees and see if that is comfortable for your back and legs. Let your feet relax outward. Meditation in this posture can be helpful if you suffer from insomnia. Practicing in bed as you prepare to sleep is a good way to deepen into a state of relaxation, releasing accumulated stress and your busy mind's activity. At some point in our lives, we may experience illness or disability. It may then become quite important to be able to meditate lying down. It is good to practice before that time.

MIX AND MATCH

As you grow in your meditation practice, you can experiment with all four postures. You may wish to alternate them on different days or combine two or more in a single practice period. You could begin with standing before a sacred image and then sitting, or if you are enjoying a long sit, you may wish to do walking meditation halfway through. There are many possibilities. Let these options nourish your experience.

THE BREATH

What is it about the breath? Over and over again, you hear the instructions to focus on the breath or return to your breath. Why is this important? The breath is the bridge between your body and mind. In many traditions, it is also connected to Spirit. It is the carrier of life. On a practical note, it is always with us. You can be on the operating table stripped of everything, but you will have your breath. Even if your breath is compromised, it is keeping you alive, and for this, you can be grateful. Turning our awareness to our breath allows us to connect to our body and its rhythm. It allows our minds to rest in this awareness and focus there. Our feelings can be observed. Our busy minds turn to this simple action of inhalation and exhalation, releasing other mental traffic, or at least part of it. In some traditions such as yoga and tai chi, you can also attach movement to the breath. But first, just make friends with your breath and observe how it can support your meditation. Here are some words from the tradition of Thich Nhất Hanh you can utilize as part of the practice.

Breathing in, I know I am breathing in.
Breathing out, I know I am breathing out.
Breathing in, my breath grows deep.
Breathing out, my breath grows slow.
Breathing in, I calm.
Breathing out, I am at ease.
Breathing in, I smile.
Breathing out, I release.
Breathing in, I know this is a precious moment.
Breathing out, this is a wonderful moment.

GUIDED AND SILENT MEDITATIONS

It may be difficult to sit in total silence at home alone. If you find it challenging, there are many resources for guided meditations. You can even create your own. Meditations are available on YouTube or from the websites of popular teachers and spiritual communities. There are CDs readily available and now apps, like Headspace or Calm, on our phones. When choosing a guided meditation, one of the most important things to consider is the voice. What one person resonates with will grate on another. This needs some investigating. You may have found a teacher that you are greatly benefiting from, but his or her voice may irritate you in some way. If patient, you will find several facilitators whose voices are helpful to your meditation. You may also explore the various themes that are available. They range from the general, such as developing compassion, to the very specific, such as overcoming addictions. Many guided meditations will include some music, or you may wish to meditate just to music. There is interesting work being done on the healing potential of sound, and there are a wide variety of recorded options. There are also recordings of nature sounds that many find helpful. If you have tinnitus (ringing in the ears), it would be wise to try some of these options as you meditate.

LOVINGKINDNESS (METTA) MEDITATION

From the Buddhist tradition, we are offered lovingkindness meditation. It is both beautiful and powerful. You will notice that it starts with yourself, then moves out to those closest to you, to acquaintances, to those who make you suffer, and finally, to the entire universe. You can think of it as waves of love and compassion directed first inward and then rippling outward. The idea of taking care of yourself first is radical for many of us, but the reasoning behind it is simple. We take care of ourselves so we can honor our own Buddha nature within, in preparation for service to others. It is like putting on your oxygen mask first on an airplane. Next, we send love where it is easiest, to those we already love. We continue with those in our life we see but do not know well and then go on to the hard part. Sending love to those who make us suffer seems almost illogical. Certainly, we can understand that we should not get vindictive or seek revenge, but couldn't we just turn our backs? This meditation teaches us that we are all so deeply connected that we cannot do that. We must seek everyone's well-being if we are to experience it ourselves. Indeed, it is in our self-interest to seek our enemies' well-being. And honestly, if he or she joins us and becomes filled with lovingkindness, wouldn't the situation change completely? Of course. But if at any time it is just too emotional and difficult to meditate on some situations, take an easier option and wait for the opening to come to your heart. We end lovingkindness meditation with a well-wishing for the entire universe. This is a blessing that goes forth from the meditator to all that is. As you practice, add individuals' names as appropriate and change the words to suit your own life. Here is a basic framework to begin.

May I be filled with lovingkindness.
May I be well.
May I be peaceful and at ease.
May I be happy, wise, and free.

May those I love be filled with lovingkindness.
May they be well.
May they be peaceful and at ease.
May they be happy, wise, and free.

May those I meet today be filled with lovingkindness.
May they be well.
May they be peaceful and at ease.
May they be happy, wise, and free.

May those who cause me suffering be filled with lovingkindness.
May they be well.
May they be peaceful and at ease.
May they be happy, wise, and free.

May the Universe be filled with lovingkindness.
May all be well.
May all be peaceful and at ease.
May all be happy, wise, and free.

CENTERING PRAYER

Fr. Thomas Keating, a Trappist monk, brought centering prayer to large numbers of Roman Catholics and other Christians. It is based on centuries of meditative Christian practices such as *Lectio Divina* and the Jesus prayer. There are four steps. First, you choose a sacred word that resonates with you. Second, you get seated, close your eyes and begin to focus on your word. Third, when thoughts arise, you gently return to your chosen word. And last of all, you end by sitting in total silence. This is not meant to replace traditional prayers but is meant as a supplement to them, a time of deep listening to the presence and word of God.

SUPPORTS

There are many things you can do to support your meditation practice. One of the most important is to establish a routine. Choose a time of day and a designated place to meditate. Of course, you can vary your routine, but it is a great help to have one. The time you choose should be when you are relaxed and the surroundings are quiet. If you need or want your meditation to be a certain number of minutes, use a timer and then release all thoughts of time. Your stomach should be nearly empty, but you do not want to be hungry. Turn off your phone and manage any other potential distractions as much as possible. You may wish to have an altar and/or some beautiful things around you for inspiration. For example, you may enjoy bells, gongs, chants, music, beads, incense, candles, or images. At times, you may incorporate movement such as yoga or tai chi. If you journal or draw, you may want to place materials near you so you can transition to those activities as you leave your meditation. Inspirational reading material may be used to begin or end your sit. On a lovely day, you may choose to sit or walk outside.

Let me take a moment to address bells. Bells have an important history in many traditions. For centuries they have called people to prayer and sounded the alarm for fire or other dangers. In Buddhism, the sound of the bell is referred to as the "voice of the Buddha." The sound calls us to stop and breathe several times, returning to the present. In meditation practice, the bell is utilized to announce the beginning, a pause, and the conclusion. It slows us down gracefully. You will see in a number of my meditations an indication to invite (never strike or hit) the bell. It is optional but well worth trying.

Prepare. That is the critical message, no matter what tools you choose to employ. This is a profound opportunity. It is important to enter your time of meditation with intention and a sense of welcome for the sacred.

If you are fortunate to belong to a nourishing spiritual community, you will find great support there. Not only does community reinforce your regular practice, but it also inspires you with the sharing that occurs naturally. You will notice that meditating in a group often elevates the experience since the collective energy of people sitting together can be strong. If you belong to a community that does not offer meditation or centering prayer, consider organizing the opportunity for all. Just as meditation centers us individually, so it can offer that grounding to a community.

As you sit, alone or with others, beware of the judging mind which likes to visit. It is just another stream of thoughts to be released. When resistance to your practice arises, sit for just a few minutes or try walking meditation. Resistance does come, and it's normal for us all, so do not let it discourage you or evoke that judging mind. Using a guided meditation can also help at these times.

When you are ready to stop meditating, slowly and gently return your awareness to your body and surroundings. Take your time making this transition from your meditation to the rest of your day or night.

THE GREATEST OBSTACLE

In my experience as a meditation teacher, the greatest obstacle to meditation is our minds. Whether it is after the first class or after a year of classes, some students give up because they feel they cannot stop their thoughts while in meditation. Of course, they can't because thoughts are the nature of the mind. This kind of harsh self-judgment is common in Western culture and to be guarded against. You may slow down your thoughts. You may experience times of no thinking or of gaps in your thoughts. But they will return. This is not failure; it is simply where your mind is at the moment. Some of us have incredibly busy brains. When we feel like failures as meditators, we need to understand that we are judging ourselves and switch to curiosity. Explore what is happening and simply note it. Just recognize, Ah, that's what's up for me today. Tomorrow will be different. The trick is to smile at it and to know that this is the nature of the experience. Strangely enough, getting upset at your thinking only strengthens it. Resistance reinforces. If you meditate for a long time, you will have many kinds of mind journeys. Some will be strange. Some will annoy you. Some will be blissful. Some will be quiet. Accept them all as they arrive and let them go. Trust your practice. Yes, tomorrow will be different.

MINDFULNESS

The Chinese character for mindfulness is made up of two separate characters. One means *now*, and the other means *heart* or *mind*. This is a good starting point for understanding mindfulness. It is being in the now, the present moment, with full attention and an open heart. Mindfulness is taking our meditation practice out into the world in our daily lives. This sounds simple enough. Most of us understand exactly what this means and are happy to be mindful. It feels good to us to be here now. But we slip out of mindfulness so easily! It is a good skill to concentrate on because it is through diligent practice that we will be able to be mindful more frequently and when we need it the most.

The Chinese poet, Chuang Tzu, wrote an enduring piece back in fourth-century BCE that demonstrates how long people have been trying to master their mental activity. This translation is by Thomas Merton. In it, we can see the clear image of an archer who loses his skill as he drifts into his thoughts. Especially seductive is the thought of competition, of winning—the fertile ground of ego.

The Need to Win
When an archer is shooting for nothing
he has all his skill.
If he shoots for a brass buckle
he is already nervous.
If he shoots for a prize of gold
He goes blind

MEDITATION AND MINDFULNESS

or sees two targets.
He is out of his mind!
His skill has not changed.
But the prize divides him.
He cares.
He thinks more of winning
than of shooting—
and the need to win
drains him of power.

Mindfulness is used by the military today to enhance fighting performance. Businesses use it to increase workers' productivity. It is effective for these purposes, but our goal is different. We are using mindfulness to gain clarity of thought and to create a pause, the pause between stimulus and response. Mindfulness helps us carefully consider our words and our actions. In this way, it can bring great improvement to our relationships with others. We are more deliberate, and because we take time to understand what is happening fully, we are more compassionate. Mindfulness is a practice of patience. It is non-judging and accepting. That does not mean that in difficult situations where harm is being done, we just let things go on. It does mean we accept reality without embellishments. And it does mean that we take the time to listen with head and heart, bringing our lovingkindness to all parties and then taking well-considered action for the greatest good.

If you are new to mindfulness, it will change your life. It is the opposite of being mindless, of living in distraction. It does not take strong effort, but it does take consistent effort. It does not mean we do not think about the past, its lessons, or our wonderful memories. But when we visit the past, we do so knowingly and with intention. We also visit the future to make necessary plans, but we do it in the same manner—consciously. To become more mindful, you may wish to put some reminders into your life. You could wear a piece of jewelry that says "breathe" or "now." Make some "breathe" signs and put them in places where you'll see them, such as your desk, bedside table, or above the kitchen sink. Stop and breathe when you hear a clock chime or the phone ring. You can set a meditation bell to ring on your computer. Three breaths will do; that is enough to bring you into the here and now. After some time, it will take no effort at all, but you will still like the reminders. Mindfulness is a skill to practice. Life only happens in the present moment. Don't miss it!

QUESTIONS FOR REFLECTION

1. Is there some new meditation practice that you would like to try? How can you make that happen?
2. Are you experiencing obstacles to your meditation practice? What changes can you make to help surmount them?
3. Would you benefit from practicing with others? See if there is a centering prayer or meditation group near you. If not, consider starting one.

CREATIVE STRETCH

1. If you can, visit a monastery and soak up the atmosphere.
2. Whatever your spiritual tradition, find a different one to visit and experience their meditative practices. You can do this as an observer or as a participant. Either way will be inspiring and feed your own practice.
3. If you have not already done so, journal and/or draw at the conclusion of your sit. Your open field of awareness will bear fruit.

A Meditation Hall Prayer

Dear Lord, teach me to meditate like a Buddha—
perfect posture, serene mind,
approaching enlightenment.

In the early morning darkness
soft candlelight and bells inspire.
The comfort of the community of sisters and brothers beckons.

Breathing in, breathing out.
Breathing in, breathing out.
Adjusting to the meditation hall.
Adjusting to my breath.

Breathing in, breathing out.
Breathing in, breathing out.
A little spider crawls in front of me.
Someone's grandfather? That seems silly, but . . .
maybe. Closing my eyes to distractions.

Breathing in, breathing out.
Breathing in, breathing out.
Sinking into my body, resting.
A sudden jerk awakens me.
Eyes open again.

Breathing in, breathing out.
Breathing in, breathing out.
The brother in front of me has strong shoulders.
Wondering . . . Whoa! It's the meditation hall.
Get a grip!

Breathing in, breathing out.
Breathing in, breathing out.
What is that pain in my side?
Where is my appendix?
Perhaps it's cancer. I may be dying. Now.

Breathing in, breathing out.
Breathing in, breathing out.
Dear Lord, calm my mind.
It is as busy as a mall on Black Friday.
Slow down, calm.

Breathing in, breathing out.
Breathing in, breathing out.
Quiet comes.
Meditation is glorious!
Judging mind. Still busy mind.

Breathing in, breathing out.
Breathing in, breathing out.
Has the sister at the bell fallen asleep?
What happens? Do we miss breakfast?

Breathing in, breathing out.
Breathing in, breathing out.
Stomach rumbles. Will there be pancakes?
Back to the present.
Cease the dreaming.

Breathing in, breathing out.
Breathing in, breathing out.
Let go of thoughts.
Let go of expectations.

The meditation is . . .
Simply is . . .

Ah, the bell.

CHAPTER THREE

SOLITUDE AND COMMUNITY

*"It is easy in the world to live after the world's opinion.
It is easy in solitude to live after your own; but the great
(wo)man is (s)he who, in the midst of the world, keeps
with perfect sweetness the independence of solitude."*
—Ralph Waldo Emerson

SOLITUDE

There is a wide range of visceral reactions to the word "solitude." For many, it brings up feelings of fear and dread. It can trigger the specters of abandonment, isolation, and death. For others, it brings the sweet relief of promised refuge, a place of quiet in a chaotic world. What does it mean to you at this point in your life? Why is it crucial?

Solitude is a pillar of spiritual life. It is necessary for anyone who wishes to live with deliberation, to live consciously no matter what is confronted. It is in solitude that we meet our true selves and that we come to understand our lives in the world. Our relationships, our work, our play, and our spirit all benefit from reflection. We can reflect with others, and at times, this is important, but we need to turn to our inner teacher first and foremost. It is there that we learn who we are and what we truly aspire to. It is there we can find our North Star, our guiding light.

There are many pressures in contemporary society. We live lives that are driven by our schedules. Being busy has come to be seen as a type of virtue and sign of self-worth. We are obsessed with speed, how fast we can drive, graduate, read, cook, or get anything done. Technology has propelled this preoccupation with time even further.

We are bombarded with a constant flow of information that we need to digest in some way. When contacting someone, we expect a response in minutes, and we feel compelled to respond to others just as quickly. Exchanges are often thoughtless and superficial; all reflection is sacrificed to this love of speed. This is a strange way to live and not one for which we were designed. We see epidemics of anxiety and depression, much of it due to these societal pressures.

Our creativity is abandoned when we deny ourselves solitude. Solitude is the great incubator of creative expression. It is often when we are alone that the tiny germs of new ideas can begin to grow. It is then that we can play with these ideas and arrange them in various formations in our minds. Images appear to inspire us, and our right brain becomes engaged. This is when the "ah-ha" moments are allowed to manifest.

Although solitude implies that we will be alone, it does not imply that we will be lonely. The ability to be alone is a life skill that we can cultivate in ourselves and others. It is something that children can be encouraged to learn to enjoy. It is unfortunate that punishment is often "time out." A break from others could better be seen as self-care, a time to rest, recharge, and reflect. Being sent to one's room for some alone time could be a blessing, not a curse. Often overscheduled, children can greatly benefit from learning to amuse themselves. Adults have an opportunity to set a good example for children in this endeavor.

Silence is another great pillar of spiritual life, and it often accompanies solitude. In the sixteenth century, John of the Cross taught, "*Silence is God's first language.*" In Buddhism, you hear the term "Noble Silence." This originates with stories of the Buddha's silent response to unanswerable questions. It has become a deep practice of individuals and communities, both Buddhist and others, to keep silent in order to help still the mind and develop increased awareness and compassion. When our words come out of a well of silence, they will be increasingly relevant, constructive, and kind. Silence can be an unexpected gift, or it may be cultivated. You may hear the terms "free silence" or "outer silence," as well as the terms "intentional silence" or "interior silence." Free or outer silence occurs when we stop the noise and let go of our minds' chatter. It can be as simple as walking into a quiet house at the end of a busy, noisy day. This gift of silence leads to a feeling of refreshment and greater clarity. Adding your intentions to that silence changes it to an experience of prayer and/or meditation. Here, in intentional or interior silence, we bring our awareness to our minds and learn to gently discourage recurring thoughts and images. We shift into a receptive mode, ready to receive whatever is offered. It is this practice of intention that deepens the experience and can lead to great insight. But keep in mind that any experience of meditation is not consistent and should not be driven by goals that lead to striving and self-judgment. Just sit with lovingkindness and curiosity. That is enough. Interestingly, silence is almost never totally silent. Ask any meditator. Some form of noise will often come and go, but hopefully, the noise is not intrusive or distracting. It is just part of our awareness to listen to the silence and hear what is there.

Our silent presence is a powerful gift we can offer to loved ones who are suffering. Too often, well-intentioned friends and family try to fix one another, offering unsolicited advice and opinions. To sit silently with anyone in pain, providing the support of your loving concern, is healing and transformative. Such support allows the sufferer to calm and tap into his or her own inner wisdom. This art of "being with" is profound.

Solitude and silence are part of many religious institutions, the mainstays of monasteries, ashrams, and other spiritual communities. They are found in hermitages and zendos and temples. Anywhere there is meditation and prayer, these pillars of spirituality can be found. Solitude and silence can also be part of a pilgrimage experience. It is a beautiful practice to designate an inspiring place to which you wish to journey and then set off, quietly and on your own, in a prayerful manner. The outer journey is simply a reflection of the inner journey. It is meant to spiritually nourish pilgrims, often connecting us to ancestors and great beings who have gone before us. Being a pilgrim can help us set a course, stay on course, or inspire our course.

For many, the solitude of nature is an evocative, elevating experience. It is here in God's great cathedral that peace is easily touched, and the fruits of spiritual practice are most directly accessed. In nature, we are never totally alone, and silence is elusive. We experience our connection to other beings through the sounds of scurrying movements, calls and songs, and momentary glimpses of tails, feathers, and wings. It is here that we can feel our connection to the web of life through all our senses. It is somehow reassuring to know we belong to the larger picture of creation. Spending time in this way helps us understand our ever-evolving role in this world. As Henry David Thoreau wrote so beautifully, "*I went to the woods because I wished to live deliberately, to front only the essential facts of life, and see if I could not learn what it had to teach, and not, when I came to die, discover that I had not lived.*"

Pilgrimages and nature may not be available to us every day, but solitude and silence await us always. If there are many responsibilities tugging at you, it may be challenging to regularly practice in solitude, but it is critical to spiritual health. How you practice may also need to change over time as your circumstances change. Be creative. It may be as simple as taking your dog for a walk or getting up a half-hour earlier while the house is still quiet. It may be a yoga class that is delivered in a meditative manner or an app for guided meditations or prayers that you can plug into each day. Readings of poetry, scripture, or other spiritual texts can also be supportive. Intentionally adding sounds such as meditative music, bells, chimes, or gongs may enrich your experience of silence and can be especially helpful for folks with hearing issues. Such sounds should be carefully curated so they do not become subjects of thought. You may wish to find a friend or small group to share your practice and to help you stay on track. Seeing a spiritual director or another counselor regularly can assist with clarifying your goals and attaining them. Swami Vivekananda tells us, "*The seeker's silence is the loudest form of prayer.*" Make silence a priority in the days you are given.

COMMUNITY

Of course, we are not meant to live totally in solitude. We are social beings and benefit greatly from our relationships. Even the most difficult ones can help us grow in compassion and understanding. They have the potential to make us stronger. Whether we gather in synagogues, churches, temples, or mosques, a community is recognized as essential to spiritual life across the wisdom traditions. It is here that we come to worship together, to learn, and to support one another. Think of a beautiful chant or hymn that uplifts you. Then think of your experience when you hear it in person, as opposed to listening to a recording. Go further by reflecting on how it feels to join your own voice to others. As we come closer and closer to participating in the actual production of sound, our spirits are lifted higher. We are stronger together. Long-time meditators will tell you that sitting with others is a different and often more powerful experience than sitting alone. Communal prayer lifts our hearts and allows us to feel our connection with those around us. Many different pathways lead to the joining of individual consciousness to the collective consciousness, which may allow us to touch transcendence.

For many, there will be more than one spiritual community, either simultaneously or over the course of a lifetime. Often there are opportunities within community life for the enjoyment of solitude and silence. They complement one another and deepen both individual and community growth.

It is an amazing experience to be at a retreat with a thousand silent people. In the tradition of Thich Nhất Hanh, there are such retreat gatherings. Typically, the retreatants wake at early light and gather outdoors for mindful movements, then do walking meditation, sitting meditation, and breakfast, all in silence. This practice in large groups creates a strong energy of community. It elevates everyone's individual practice. However, groups do not have to be large to have an impact. If you are a yogi, you have experienced the difference between the beauty of a solitary practice and the beauty of joining in with others. Both are valid and important for realizing our human potential.

How do we choose a community? How do we know who will be a great teacher for us? These are critical questions for us all.

CONSIDERATIONS WHEN CHOOSING A SPIRITUAL TEACHER

There are a number of considerations when you are looking to learn and deepen your spiritual life through a religious leader. The first thing to reflect on is exactly what are you seeking? Are you looking for a teacher, a role model, a companion, or a guide? Do you want someone to instruct you in a particular religion, to guide you in spiritual practices, or someone who can help you grow in awareness? What are your goals? Do they involve others, such as family members?

As you look at the possibilities, inquire about who each person is. What is his or her history, training, and what do others have to say? You can do a lot of research online. What does this teacher expect from you? Create your own high standards and look for someone who offers you the respect you deserve as an adult seeker. Is this teacher open to other traditions and leaders? Does this teacher embody joy? In my experience, the most spiritually evolved people radiate joy. Look for it.

Remember, no matter who you choose, this is a human being full of flaws and frailties. Mistakes will be made, and there will be plenty of opportunities to be offended and even hurt. What is important is not perfection (which is impossible) but integrity. In daily life, does this person reflect the values that are espoused? Are missteps shared and learned from? That said, if you feel uncomfortable with someone at any level, please put your energy into moving on and continuing to look for the right religious leader for you.

Know that you can have more than one teacher simultaneously and over time. If someone tells you otherwise, that is a red flag. The most important teacher is your own inner teacher. Buddha's words remain instructive: "*Be a lamp unto yourself. Betake yourselves to no exalted refuge. Hold fast to the truth.*" You can benefit greatly from others, but never underestimate the wisdom held within your own life experience.

CONSIDERATIONS WHEN CHOOSING A SPIRITUAL COMMUNITY

Once you are clear about what kind of community you are seeking, it is time to look at what is available. Geography can be restrictive. There are virtual communities for those comfortable with that option, but there are limitations to what can be offered via technology. On the other hand, especially for those who have been wounded in spiritual communities, this might be a comfortable option. If possible, visit any local or regional organization you are interested in joining to learn more about them. If such a request is denied, be sure to ask why and when you would be able to observe them.

Assess if the teachings are in accordance with your own beliefs. This can be done through direct contact or reading books, websites, or public information literature. It is a good idea to get an understanding of how this group is organized. Is there strong leadership resting in an individual or a small group, or is there wide participation in governance? What are you comfortable with? Is there transparency in the decision-making process and conflict resolution? What are the expectations of members? What demands are made on time, talent, and treasure? What are you able and willing to offer to meet any such expectations?

You may feel that you have no idea what to expect or what would suit you. In that case, talk to like-minded friends and see what their experiences have been. Try to visit several organizations and experience their cultures. What suits one person may not suit another. That is one reason for the emergence of many different types of religious groups. Some people want to have a highly intellectual experience, while others look for the celebration of traditional rituals, a strong arts presence, or quality children's programming. Perhaps you have an interest in social justice, so you would benefit from that type of opportunity. In some communities, there is a lot of socializing, and in others, hardly any. You might need to belong to more than one organization. That is perfectly fine. Perhaps the most important feeling you should experience in any religious community is a sense of homecoming. Keep looking until you find a community where you feel you belong.

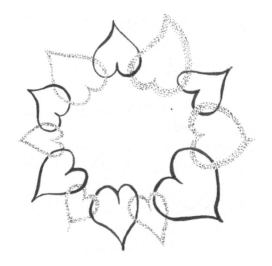

QUESTIONS FOR REFLECTION

1. What thoughts and/or feelings do these words evoke for you?
   Silence Solitude Stillness Groups Community
2. Meister Eckhart tells us, *"Nothing is so like God as silence."* What have been your experiences of silence throughout your life? Positive? Negative? Try to give specific examples reaching all the way back to childhood.
3. Do you experience silence and solitude each day?
4. Do you sometimes avoid silence or being alone? When? Do you know why?
5. What have been your experiences of spiritual communities throughout your life? Have you experienced any spiritual wounding in community? Have you been nourished? Again, reach all the way back to your childhood and reflect on your personal history.
6. What communities do you belong to now? Do they enhance your life?
7. Do you have particular interests that would be well served by group support? Can you find such a community or start one?

CREATIVE STRETCH

1. Attend a silent retreat for a day, weekend, week, month, or longer. Decide on a time commitment that is comfortable for you and allows for a positive experience. Different traditions offer a variety of schedule options (worship, teaching, meditation, spiritual direction, consultations, free time, and more). Do your research and find a program that suits your needs and wishes.
2. Do you have a goal that would benefit from group support? Perhaps you would like to read a certain religious text or establish a spiritual practice. Find a few like-minded souls and offer to organize gatherings. This is a great way to deepen friendships as well as learn.

3. What is your relationship to nature? How is it incorporated into your life? Thomas Merton reminds us, "No *writing on the solitary meditative life can say anything that has not already been said better by the wind in the pine trees.*" Explore and expand your friendship with the natural world.

A Morning Meditation

In the early hours of the day
it is possible to enter a place
between worlds.
As the approaching dawn is
not yet day, and no longer night,
I am not yet in this world,
but in a dimension invisible.

I stand at the threshold of my heart.
Deep in its inner chambers
is a hearth.
There rests the spark of Divine Light.
Slowly, carefully I look at the
heart's chambers.
What is my reality at this time of beginning?

There is beauty to behold.
Love given and received, again and again.
There is clutter to attend to,
sweeping out misdirections, clinging, and mindlessness.
And there are stains and soil to cleanse—
hurts, grudges, narrowness of thoughts
and darkness of fears.

Let me rest here.
Let me see my new day wisely.
Letting go.
Resolving.
Appreciating.
Feeling gratitude.
Knowing love.
(Bell—a period of silence)

Refreshed by the night's healing
I turn and face the world.
I am on a new threshold,
one of potential—known and unknown—
of limitless possibilities.
I step into the day with joy
and yes, with courage.

Who shall cross my path today?
What events will occur?
May I greet all as teachers
and may I love with generosity.
May my heart sing with praise
for all creation.
May I breathe in peace.

Teach me to live in harmony
with all that is.
Teach me to serve all that
comes before me.
Teach me to live deliberately
and joyfully.
Teach me to be the Divine Light within.
(Bell 3x)

CHAPTER FOUR

FORGIVENESS

*"Holding resentment is like eating poison and waiting for the
other person to keel over."*
—Author Unknown

All of us experience anger and resentment directed toward
those who have wronged us. We also acknowledge we have
hurt and failed others. We recognize what it is to harm ourselves. This is our flawed humanity. We cannot totally rid ourselves
of our imperfections. The question is, what do we do with the resulting feelings of sadness, anger, resentment, guilt, and shame? Do we
hang on to them for dear life, or do we release them in forgiveness?
If we want to live in peace, it is necessary to forgive and to be forgiven. We can learn to do both through spiritual practice.

It is critical to recognize what forgiveness is not. Forgiveness is not
approval. It does not excuse. It is not permission to continue hurtful
behavior. Forgiveness does not mean forgetting. It may, or may not,
mean reconciliation. Ultimately, forgiveness is the gaining of wisdom
and the healing of your heart. Nothing more and nothing less.

So why do we resist forgiveness? Why do we nurture our
grudges and revel in our anger? Part of the answer to this can be
felt in our bodies. Think of something that really angers you and
see if you can note any physical changes. Do you feel a surge of
energy or racing of your heart? The reward our anger gives us is
this feeling of power, of strength. Of course, it is not real power
but a surge in energy that creates that sensation. Our resent-
ments also may bestow on us self-righteous feelings and a sense
of superiority to others. These strokes to our ego reinforce our
negative attitudes. They may be subtle, but you can get in touch

with these thoughts and feelings. Then the option of wisely shifting your experience opens up.

We also resist the process of forgiveness because it makes us feel vulnerable. Indeed, we are opening our hearts and minds as we explore our difficulties. We may be hurt. We may be culpable in some way. Vulnerability is uncomfortable, and we naturally try to avoid it, but in this case, vulnerability leads to increased strength if we can find the courage to proceed. Forgiveness is an act of courage, not for the faint of heart.

What are the benefits of forgiveness? The many benefits include better heart health and lower blood pressure, reduced stress and anxiety, cased depression, a stronger immune system, and of course, better relationships and peace of mind. Spiritually we are stuck when we hold on to any bitterness toward others or ourselves. We close our hearts and become limited in our life of prayer and meditation. Our divine nature becomes clouded in our own perception. Our divine spark dims. Beyond our individual interests, a global reduction in the energies of hostility has profound effects on the world. Each day we all contribute to those global energies in a positive or negative way. The choice is ours.

As a spiritual practice, forgiveness requires a regular commitment to healing the smallest transgressions. This ongoing practice will support us when a big crisis arrives, as it inevitably does in life. Many of us will remember being deeply moved as the Amish of Nickel Mines, Pennsylvania, arrived in a parade of horse-drawn buggies to the funeral of Charles Roberts IV, who had killed ten of their children, precious little girls, just days before. How could this be? How could they attend his funeral, visit his parents, and pray for him? In part, the answer lies in the fact that the Amish begin practicing forgiveness regularly as children. It is ingrained in their lifestyle. So when this tragedy arrived, they were able to do what seemed beyond human, but was for them a deeply Christian response. We can all learn to give and receive forgiveness. It requires our commitment to its value, a life of daily reflection, and a willingness to be vulnerable.

You may feel like this is just too hard. What has happened to you or what you have done to another is just too big to be forgiven. But all can be forgiven; it is within our power. What may be needed is some support from others. There are a number of options: retreats or workshops on forgiveness, excellent books, therapists, life coaches, spiritual directors, clergy, or a trusted friend to companion you through your process. You may also find inspiration and support from those you have witnessed forgiving well. To forgive well means to forgive with your whole heart, not just verbally, while still retaining ill will. You may know someone who has set a great example for you. If not, you can learn about public figures who have much to teach us about forgiveness. There are many examples, but here are just a few. Robbie Parker's six-year-old daughter was killed at Sandy Hook Elementary School. Just hours later, he stood before the television cameras, forgave the shooter, and offered condolences to his family. Nelson Mandala served twenty-seven years as a political prisoner in South Africa. He forgave those who imprisoned him and went on to become president of his country. Certainly, his pathway to success was cleared by his ability to forgive and move on. And going back to ancient times, in the Orthodox Christian traditions, one can be inspired by the amazing life of the saint of penitents, Mary of Egypt.

Our perceptions are always limited. It is helpful to remember this. If we are seated at a table looking at a vase of flowers, what each of us sees is the same bouquet, yet different. We all look from our own position, and the view varies with each seat. This is true of our lives in general. But we can aim to expand our vision while understanding that it will never be complete. What is your point of view? What is the point of view of others? There is a gem of a little book by Henri Nouwen entitled, *The Return of the Prodigal Son*. In it, the theologian explores Rembrandt's masterpiece of the same title and his relationship to it. He looks at the familiar story of the lost son, the faithful son, and the forgiving father, identifying with each of the figures. This is a process we can apply to any situation that needs forgiveness. Try to imagine seeing from the vantage point of each person involved. It will expand awareness and help direct you toward healing.

THE BUDDHIST PRACTICE OF BEGINNING ANEW

In the Buddhist community of Thich Nhất Hanh, there is a forgiveness practice called Beginning Anew. Participants are practitioners who have experience in meditation, deep listening, and mindfulness, which are helpful to the process. The brothers and sisters who are feeling some upset sit together and follow the guidelines with care. Often they invite a senior member of the *sangha* (community) to sit with them and help guide the process. It is also possible to follow the steps on your own. You can begin anew with someone, and they need not even be aware. Anyone can benefit from learning how. These are the four steps.

1. Flower Watering: This first step is a game changer. You are asked to share an appreciation of the other person. What trait in this person do you truly admire? Or perhaps there was a specific situation where the person showed strength or positive quality that you can recollect. Reflecting on the positive qualities of any individual can help shift your perspective. You remember that the person is much more than any single word or action.
2. Sharing Regrets: You apologize for any unskillfulness on your part.
3. Expressing a Hurt: This is your opportunity to explain how you feel hurt by the other person. It is good to speak from your own experience only, putting everything in "I" terms.
4. Sharing a Long-term Difficulty and Asking for Support: This step allows us to share any difficulties in our life that are continuing. These issues that we are practicing with can help others understand us better and know how to offer their support.

Beginning Anew allows those participating to talk to one another by taking turns without any interruptions. Buddhists are taught to listen deeply without judgment and to be kind in speech. It is a deep and powerful practice that can benefit us all.

A Buddhist Prayer of Forgiveness
If I have harmed anyone in any way, either knowingly or unknowingly
through my own confusions, I ask their forgiveness.
If anyone has harmed me in any way, either knowingly or unknowingly
through their own confusions, I forgive them.
And if there is a situation I am not yet ready to forgive
I forgive myself for that.
For all the ways that I harm myself, negate, doubt, belittle myself,
judge, or am unkind to myself through my own confusions,
I forgive myself.

PENANCE IN THE CHRISTIAN TRADITION

For Christians, there is a third party to consider when seeking forgiveness: God. In Protestant churches, women and men make their confessions of sins directly to God through prayer. This is seen as a personal matter between the person and his or her maker. Churches in the orthodox traditions offer the sacrament of reconciliation or the sacred mystery of confession. This sacrament has several steps: examination of conscience, sincere remorse, confession of sins to a priest, absolution, and penance, which is usually prayer but may also include some form of restitution. It is believed that through this sacrament, sins are forgiven, and the right relationship with God is reestablished. The role of the priest is one of intermediary and guide, but forgiveness comes from God. This is a healing of one's rift with the Divine because of sin. It may or may not address fractured relationships with other people or situations.

This sacrament has the potential to be emotionally powerful for participants. It can lead to a strong sense of relief with the release of guilt and shame. It can also be difficult for some people who are painfully hard on themselves. Some may also fall into the trap of becoming overly scrupulous. But for those for whom this sacrament is a blessing, it brings a lightness of heart and a welcome new beginning.

ATONEMENT IN JUDAISM

Yom Kippur is a period of fasting, prayer, and atonement that occurs each autumn for those of the Jewish faith. In this tradition, no intermediary is required for God to offer forgiveness. But first, one must apologize and seek forgiveness from anyone who has been hurt. Only then will the prayers of Yom Kippur effectively remove sins.

Interestingly, Yom Kippur prayers recognize collective as well as individual responsibility for transgressions. Notice the use of the pronoun "we" in this excerpt.

For the sin which we have committed in Your sight through arrogance of our will,
and for the sin which we have committed before You by breach of trust.
For the sin which we have committed in Your sight by casting off responsibility,
and for the sin which we have committed before You by denying and lying.
For the sin which we have committed in Your sight by evil thoughts,
for all of these, O God of forgiveness,
forgive us, pardon us, grant us atonement.

One of the most beautiful forgiveness prayers ever written comes from the Jewish tradition. It is known as the Ravensbruck Prayer and was found at Ravensbruck concentration camp, where 92,000 women and children died in World War II. It was scrawled on wrapping paper near a dead child. The author is unknown.

> Lord, remember not only the men and women of good will, also those of ill will.
> But do not only remember the suffering they have inflicted on us.
> Remember the fruits we have brought, thanks to this suffering—our comradeship, our loyalty, our humility, the courage, the generosity, the greatness of heart which has grown out of all this.
> And when they come to judgment, let all the fruits we have borne be their forgiveness.
> Amen.

ASKING FOR FORGIVENESS

It can be extraordinarily difficult to ask someone to forgive us. The larger the transgression, the harder it is. Asking is humbling, and we cannot be sure of the reaction that might be evoked. But to live at peace with ourselves, much less others, apologies are required. So, the time comes when we must gather our courage and ask for forgiveness. This is most powerful if done in person, but if that is not possible, it may be done in writing. If the person is no longer alive, a letter addressed to him or her is still a good way to reflect on the situation. Here are seven steps to guide you.

1. Acknowledge the Transgression: First of all, we must admit to ourselves that we failed in some way. Be clear about what went wrong and face it squarely. It is tempting to deny or avoid our problems, but this creates an uneasy conscience and steals our inner peace.
2. Beneficial Regret vs. Guilt and Shame: Beneficial regret is when we recognize that we did something wrong, and we learn from the experience. There are always lessons in our mistakes, and when we take them in, we can often avoid repeating the missteps.

Guilt also is feeling sorry for our thoughts, words, or deeds, but it is carried to an extreme. When we suffer from guilt, we are in an endless loop of self-recrimination. This is not helpful. Shame is the experience of regret too but includes embarrassment before others, which is also not productive. Certainly we need to feel remorse when we are responsible for hurt of any kind, but we do not need to feel it endlessly or publicly. Damaging ourselves is not going to undo the wrong and might lead to greater problems.

3. Confession or Counseling: For some people, it might be helpful or even necessary to go to confession or to seek counseling of some kind. Others might wish to have a heart-to-heart conversation with a trusted friend. Whatever steps can bring healing should be taken.

4. Apologize: Time to say you are sorry, hopefully in person, but if not, in writing.

5. Making Reparations: If possible, find a concrete way to make the situation better. If you cannot do it with the person directly involved, do it for someone else in a way that relates to the situation. For instance, if you hurt a child but you no longer know where that child lives, find a way to help another child. It will bring you peace.

6. Get Some Perspective: It is good to remember that although you failed in this particular instance, you have done many good deeds. Recall some of them and know that this goodness exists in you and is your strength. Build on it, and keep your difficulties in perspective.

7. Let Go! Last of all, when you have learned the lessons of your transgression and done all you can to make the situation better, let it go. Forgive yourself and put your energy into good works moving forward. What happened is in the past, and it is time to look to the future as a wiser person.

BEYOND THE PERSONAL

Just as individuals forgive one another, so communities also are called to forgive. These may be small neighborhood-based communities or large communities of nations, tribes, races, religions, or other organizations. This important topic is not going to be addressed here except on the level of our individual participation. Hatred is often generational and fueled by cultures. It is in stories, songs, literature, art, and dinner table conversations. It can include outright fighting or more subtle harm through prejudice expressed in endless ways.

What did you learn on your father's knee? I learned to hate the British since my Irish family knew all the stories of seven hundred years of subjugation. My heroes were others' terrorists. There is often a fine line between freedom fighters and terrorists, and we need to understand these perceptions. Even while studying in Great Britain as a young woman, I held everyone at a bit of a distance, looking at it all with curiosity but not warmth or openness. It took me years to come to understand the nature of my own prejudice and the need for forgiveness of myself and others.

Peace between nations does not have a chance if individuals do not do this work. It matters not at all if concords or treaties are signed if the people—individual by individual—do not support them. If we grew up thinking of a group of people as evil and destructive, we need to look at those feelings and how they contribute to the larger social consciousness that influences us all. We can acknowledge that harm that has been done, learn the lessons that are involved, forgive, and move on. What you do is important, even though you are only one person.

A FORGIVENESS PROCESS FOR ALL

Here is a forgiveness process that anyone can do. You may wish to do it alone or with a friend or counselor. It can be helpful to have someone else's perspective and the support of a compassionate presence. In this exercise, you are also encouraged to invoke a spiritual guide not physically present but in your consciousness. You can easily adapt it to situations that are not specific to an individual (asking forgiveness of Mother Earth, for example) or for the important practice of forgiving yourself. Often forgiveness takes a significant amount of time. You may find you need to repeat this process more than once.

- Find a quiet place and a time when you will not be uninterrupted. Consider outdoor as well as indoor options.
- If you wish, light a candle. Fire is a symbol of transformation, and you are embarking on a journey of transformation from ill-will to blessing.
- Think of someone, living or dead, whom you greatly admire for his or her ability to forgive. This may be someone you know personally or a public figure, such as the Dalai Lama, Jesus, or Viktor Frankl. Invoke this person's presence as your spiritual guide. Such a strong example of lovingkindness will support and inspire you.
- Now bring to mind the situation you would like to heal. Who do you need to forgive? Bring that person's countenance before you, and look into his or her eyes. Sit quietly for a few minutes.
- Causing you hurt is only a part of this person's life. He or she is much more than that. If possible, bring to mind one of his/her positive qualities. Reflect on this goodness. If the individual is not personally known to you, try to touch the suffering that created his or her woundedness.
- Now recall the cause of your hurt. Take time to express it to yourself in clear terms. What are the facts? Exactly what was done or not done; what was said or not said? Are you adding a story to the experience? Try to stay with what you actually know.
- Are you sure? Ask yourself this question several times. Seek clarity.
- Is it possible to imagine yourself in the offender's position? Does this bring any insight?

- Now turn your attention to the spiritual guide you have asked to support you. Request the gift of wisdom. Receive. From this higher perspective, what are you able to understand? What is your own role in this disharmony?
- If boundaries are needed to move forward, what do they look like? Does the nature of the relationship need to change? Feel safe.
- Now, if you are able, open your heart and offer total forgiveness. If you are not yet able, be kind to yourself and accept that. Simply repeat this process at intervals that feel right until your heart heals. Seek additional support if you feel stuck.
- If needed, forgive yourself for any anger or resentment you have been holding.
- Thank the person you have forgiven for any life lessons you have learned through this challenging experience.
- Thank your spiritual guide.
- Sit in silence for a while and slowly return to your day, lighter and happier.

QUESTIONS FOR REFLECTION

1. On this day, do I treasure the gift of my life?
2. Have I harmed anyone, any living being, or the earth today?
3. Have I failed to say or do anything today that causes me regret?
4. Have I been kind to myself and others?
5. Have I practiced gratitude?
6. Have I chosen joy?
7. Does anything remain unforgiven in me today?

CREATIVE STRETCH

1. Write a letter to someone expressing your regret and asking for forgiveness. Or, write a letter to someone expressing your hurt and offering your forgiveness. Sit with your letter for a period of time that feels right, and then decide to send it or destroy it. Either decision is fine. The process itself is clarifying and healing.
2. When you are trying to understand a resentment building within your heart, journal about it daily to gain insight. Reread your entries, observing any shift in perspective that may occur.
3. Consider making something with your own hands as a way to offer forgiveness or to ask for it. A meaningful photograph, a pair of socks, a loaf of bread, a painting, a poem, or any other creative expression can help heal ruptures in relationships.

A Meditation on Forgiveness

For every unkind word I have said about myself, to myself
   I open my heart in love and forgiveness.

For every wrong choice that has caused harm to my body, soul, or mind,
   I open my heart in love and forgiveness.

For every thought that has belied my sacred nature,
   I open my heart in love and forgiveness.

For every blindness to my limitless potential,
   I open my heart in love and forgiveness.

For every failure to recognize I am a channel of Divine energy,
   I open my heart in love and forgiveness.

For every unkind word I have spoken of another,
   I open my heart in love and forgiveness.

For every word of praise, encouragement, or comfort I have failed to utter,
   I open my heart in love and forgiveness.

For every instance of blindness to the Divine nature of all that is,
   I open my heart in love and forgiveness.
   For each and every tendency toward separation:
   separation from my true nature,
   separation from the love of self and others,
   separation from my connection to all that is.

I open my heart and wrap myself in compassion.
I open my heart and wrap humanity in compassion.

I open my heart and wrap Mother Earth in compassion.
I open my heart and wrap the Universe in compassion.
I forgive. (Bell)
I forgive. (Bell)
I offer unconditional, unceasing compassion and forgiveness.
(Bell 3x)

CHAPTER FIVE

CREATED TO CREATE

"It is blasphemous for any of us to say 'I am not creative.' All we do is create ... We wake up every day to an empty canvas of twenty-four hours and every night we go to bed having created our masterpiece for the day. We can do this consciously or unconsciously, but we do it nevertheless. And the ones who are conscious of it are the ones most actively engaged in the work of evolution, of unification, of ongoing cosmic revelation."
—Jan Phillips

C reativity is the generative power of the convergence of heart, mind, and soul. It celebrates what is good, beautiful, and true. And when we are faced with problems, our creative imagination joins our intellect to offer original solutions. It can be seen when we build bridges, sculpt, add a new ingredient to a recipe, or plant a garden. It is a feature of humanity that can be used for good or evil purposes. We are designed to be creators, and how we employ that gift is up to us.

Through the arts, our creativity becomes a powerful means of communication. Creativity may use words but also goes beyond them and expands language to images and sounds. It connects us across nationalities, cultures, socio-economic groups, religions, gender identities, and age classifications. The experience of creating is also an internal communication. It is a dialogue within the self that reveals our true nature and helps us stay faithful to our deepest longings, our dreams, and aspirations. It supports our integrity and points us in the direction of the manifestation of our fullest potential, created by the Divine.

The arts open up our world of experience. Art and artifacts are our first window into the history of humanity. They give us a unique view into the past, reaching back 100,000 years in the case of ocher and rock symbols discovered in South Africa. The cave drawings of France, the kerbstones of Newgrange, the pyramids of Egypt, and the ancient temples of Asia all present us with images and symbols that reflect our species' striving for understanding. We can see this engagement with the cosmos and the natural world on earth. We can also see engagement with the mystery of humankind's place in it all. This longing for understanding, this spiritual longing, is at the root of all religions.

The arts, current or past, are the expression of a process of discovery. They are a unifying human experience common to us all. At their ultimate, the arts are messengers of wisdom, justice, and compassion across time and space. Throughout history, they have been utilized to teach, preach, comfort, and uplift. The arts take many forms: drawing, painting, music, sculpture, collage, dance, storytelling, photography, film, theater, architecture, writing, needle arts, culinary arts, gardening, and more.

MISDIRECTED CREATIVITY

Used as propaganda, the arts can be a tool of separation and discrimination. The designation of propaganda is a value judgment made by both artists and consumers of the arts. One person's propaganda may be another person's art. However, this potential for employing creativity for nefarious purposes is an important awareness to maintain. Fortunately, most often, the arts are bridges for all of humanity. When we listen to a symphony or look at a masterpiece of visual art, we are brought together in a shared experience of beauty and emotion across all boundaries.

TRANSCENDENCE THROUGH THE ARTS

Spiritually, through the arts, we can touch transcendence. They help us enter union with each other and the Divine. They elevate us to heights of beauty and hope. They heal. The arts offer many pathways to the mystical. Through our imaginations and meditative practices, we connect to the invisible world. The symbol of the cross predates Christianity and is an early expression of humanity's sacred longing. If we are living in the horizontal, earth-based realm of the cross, we can also live in the vertical, transcendent dimension. Through art, we are led to looking and listening deeply. Our concentration becomes a contemplative process, meditative and powerful. A piece of music, a story, or a fine painting may be our pathway to transcendence at any time. The process of creating these art forms provides other powerful routes to transcendence. There are many choices.

FANS, SUPPORTERS, AND CREATORS

We can enter the stream of creativity in three ways. All three are important, enriching possibilities: as a fan, a supporter, and a creator. Being a fan of a field of art, a place of art, or a particular artist, is a great way to grow in our own identity as a creative person. When you were young, you may have had actors or singers you honored with endless playing of their songs or movies. You may have adorned your room with posters celebrating them. This enthusiasm for the creative expression of another person is part of falling in love with all the arts. It is an acknowledgment of their power in our lives. Whoever elevates your spirit, Yo-Yo Ma, your yoga teacher, or Meryl Streep, is your guide to an active, artistic life.

The second role is that of supporter. This can be done financially; perhaps the first idea that comes to mind with the word "support." But it can also be accomplished in a number of other ways. Importantly, the arts open up the world to the young. Through supporting their entry into the arts, we help them increase their available avenues of self-expression as well as cultivate various appreciations and intellectual growth. It certainly is easier for some children than others to visit museums, galleries, gardens, take dance classes, buy a camera, or learn to play a musical instrument. Donations and volunteers are critical, especially in schools that have few resources to provide such essentials as instruments, art, or theater materials. In difficult financial times, many schools cut back or eliminate art and music classes.

How we interact with young people is critical to their development as creators. It is easy to offer snap judgments, grades, and opinions. This can be deadening to their tender expressions of themselves. Who are we to do that, anyway? And yet, it is so common. We want children to conform to our ideas, to learn what we know. Some of that is valuable, of course, but not at the expense of the opening of imaginations and encouragement of exploration. The development of brave, creative minds is good for us as individuals and as a society. Simple, judgment-free queries are all that is needed. *What are you making? Tell me about this. How did you think of that? What does this remind you of?* Open up the conversation in a way that honors the effort, recognizes the potential, and celebrates the uniqueness of the child. This is the respectful way to talk to anyone, of any age, about their creativity.

We can also be a supporter by giving our time and talents to art institutions in our communities who so often are operating on a shoestring budget. Volunteer as a docent, an educator, a host or hostess, an usher, a ticket salesperson, a gardener, an office aide, an event planner, a caterer, or a parking lot attendant. So many ways to help!

The last way to enter this stream of consciousness is the most direct route. Honor your own identity as a creator. In the United States, this can be challenging because we live in an age of specialization that separates us in so many ways. We are taught that artists are gifted people who have extraordinary talents that make them different and beyond our understanding. But we are all gifted. The Kabbalah teaches that "*the fierce power of imagination is a gift of God.*" That power is within us all.

In the Hindu-Javanese culture of Bali, there are no words for art or artist. Traditionally, art is so thoroughly woven throughout the lives of its people that it cannot be separated. All the community is involved in the making of art in various forms such as sculpture, painting, flower arranging, dance, theater, and food preparation. These activities are part of their daily devotional practices and express their deep connections to nature, the gods, and community. Sadly, as the West impacts this country, their way of life is changing. We remain a long way from their understanding of our intrinsic creative nature as humans. It is worth holding up Bali's traditional culture as a shining example of what is possible.

So many people who say they are not creative are blind to their own creative life. This is a matter of labeling. Do you enjoy preparing a beautiful, delicious meal, planting a garden, or taking photographs? Can you see endeavors such as these as art forms? Is there something you do where time slips away and you are "in the zone"? Examine that activity for its artistic identity. All artistic endeavors are naturally mindful. Honor your creative spirit. That honoring will help it grow and bring more of your potential to full fruition.

The first two ways of participating in the arts will support this third path too. When I trained as a docent at the Hyde Collection, the curator told our class that if we were painters, the time we spent looking at the art and sharing it with visitors would help our own work. This proved to be true for me. As I studied the artworks, I saw them more clearly. I saw colors that I had not noticed before. I saw the artists' hands in fast, rough lines and in meticulous, intricate details. I noticed what works drew me in and held my attention and what ones did not. Those works opened my eyes to possibilities as I took up my own paintbrush. Something I create opens up someone else's artistic experience. Fans, supporters, and artists relate to nurturing, evolving relationships.

Just as solitary time is important to the creative life, so is community. You may wish to take a class, join a group, or organize one. There is helpful instruction, feedback, and social support at your fingertips. You can share music, readings, and exhibits. Dive into discussions of everyone's work. We get great ideas from one another, and friends along the way just make life more fun.

NURTURING OUR INNER CREATOR

Here are some tips for setting your expressive self free. It is easy to give up, to turn away, to make excuses, to drift. The following ideas will help you get back on track.

- Do the work. Treat it like a job and schedule time on your calendar to create. Make it a priority.
- Before you begin working, say a prayer or meditate. Set your intention for the time and the work. You may wish to invoke saints or angels to guide you. There might be some that are directly related to what you are expressing. Call on them.

For example, when painting an Irish landscape, I might choose Brigid and say something this simple: *"Brigid, please enter my mind, my heart, and my hands. Thank you."*

Pausing in this manner centers one and invites a meditative tone for the period of work.

- Keep all your materials at hand. If you put your yarn in a closet, you might go a long time before getting it out. When your knitting is next to your chair, you will reach for it and create your art.
- Be clear about what messages you want to send out into the world. Remember that all creative works are forms of communication. What are you trying to say?
- When your inner critic appears, turn the channel. The thoughts that flow through your mind are yours to direct. All too often, our thoughts are negative judgments we would never inflict on any friend. You deserve better. Don't put up with self-destructive nonsense!
- If something isn't working out, try something else. Change the theme or the media. Write a different chapter and return to the difficult section later.

- If things are still not working out, it is okay to decide to junk your work. Some meals aren't worth serving, and some canvases just need to be discarded.
- If you have a dry spell, know that it is part of the creative process. It is the silent, still winter of your efforts. Spring will burst forth in due time. Getting anxious about dry spells only interferes with the needed dormant phase.
- Share your work process with positive people who support you. If you don't have such a circle, start a group of like-minded creators.
- Do not entertain nay-sayers. Your work is sacred, and you need to respect boundaries that protect your efforts and your inner life.
- Take time to learn about the lives and work of those in your field. It is so encouraging, and you will gain important knowledge about the work, as well as inspiration.
- You do not have to limit yourself to one field of creative expression. In this age of specialization, we have become used to placing ourselves in isolating boxes. Don't. If you want to paint and dance, do it. If you want to write and play the violin—great!
- Try to always work from your soul. Create out of your passion and not out of your need for money or approval. If you are seeking to make a living at your work, you need to be responsive to public demand, but keep your heart involved. If those results don't sell, create for your living, but also create a different body of work for yourself. You'll never regret it.

Find ways to share the fruits of your creative efforts with others. Let your many gifts grace the world! Thomas Berry calls the universe "*the primary artist.*" You are an important part of our evolving universe and carry the identity of "artist" as your birthright. Claim it, celebrate it, and come into all your own glorious fullness of life!

QUESTIONS FOR REFLECTION

1. Am I expressing myself in creative ways? If not, why not?
2. Is there an art form that I have been wanting to try but have not yet? Why am I waiting? Am I afraid? Too busy? Could I sign up for a class or a short workshop? Where can I get support?
3. Do I need more solitude to create? Do I need a community where I can share my creativity?
4. What am I most passionate about? How can I express it?
5. How do I support the arts in my community?
6. How do I encourage young people to see themselves as creative?

CREATIVE STRETCH

1. Remember when you were a child with a wild, active imagination? Think back and see if you can recall what set it off. Make a list. Although you have changed, that child remains within you. What touched that spark in you so many years ago may do so again today. Explore your history.
2. Julia Cameron offers a fruitful practice called "artist dates." This includes taking time regularly to go off on your own to places that nurture your artistic spirit. Some that I have found helpful are gardens, garden centers, country or city walks, museums, galleries, craft centers, places of worship (especially when empty and quiet), concert halls, and any place where there are animals to observe. Enter this time with an open mind and heart. Have clear aspirations. Enjoy the experience as a meditation. Your imagination will be fed.
3. In the Middle Ages, pilgrims used to take along a *vade mecum* for company. It is a book of art, poetry, prayers, quotes, or any uplifting material. Make your own *vade mecum* of favorite images and words. It will be a source of comfort, deep joy, and inspiration.

The Bud

In the dark core of my being is an ever-greening bud.
It is rooted in the Divine, an eternally spiraling energy
of beauty, love, joy, and freedom.
It is with me always, greening in winter, glowing in darkness.
Let me claim each pulse, each messenger.
Let me not turn away in fear or distraction.
Let me understand my call to be my true self.
Let me create.
Let me speak, paint, dance, sing, write, live, and love,
in harmony with the One who sent me.

CHAPTER SIX
SAVING MOTHER EARTH

*"Of one thing we may be sure: the human community
and the natural world will go into the future as a single
sacred community or we will both experience disaster."*
—Thomas Berry

W e are of the cosmos, made of stardust. Our bodies are made up of the same four elements that appear in all material reality: fire, water, air, and earth. Our bones are of the earth; the heat of our bodies reflects our fire; the greatest portion of our mass is water, and our breath is air. We have come to think of ourselves as separate, superior beings. This ruinous misconception has allowed us to see ourselves as masters of the planet. Sadly, some philosophical and religious traditions have promoted the idea that all of creation exists in service to humankind. This flawed teaching has led to devastating levels of exploitation, and the results are inexorably rolling in.

We are living in a time when the future of our species and the entire planet is in peril. Climate change is real, as are the needs of the world's growing population. We have been borrowing against the future, and this option is no longer tenable. Entire species of plants and animals are dying off at a high, rapid rate, and yet we depend on biodiversity. Food and water supplies are increasingly threatened, and natural habitat is vanishing. There are theories and programs aiming to turn this dangerous predicament around. We need to learn all we can so we move forward in a balanced, sustainable manner. This includes our relationships to businesses as owners, employees, and consumers. It also includes worldwide social justice issues and especially the protection of our home, Mother Earth. How do we mobilize in significant enough numbers, with enough force, to make effective change possible? The answer must be found not only in our intellects but in our hearts.

Our experience of creation is Divinely sourced. It calls us to honor manifestation: animal, plant, and mineral. Some aspects might be easier than others; you might adore your pet pup but find it harder to warm up to a spider or a skunk. A lack of personal attachment does not interfere with our ability to wonder at all creatures, at their uniqueness, ingenuity, and beauty. The same is true of the wider environmental setting. Given a choice, one of us might prefer spending a day at the ocean, another in a city, and yet another in the mountains. All are treasures. All deserve our dedicated care, regardless of our predilections.

A BIT OF HISTORY

It can be helpful to look at the arc of history. The Big Bang occurred over 13 billion years ago, and the earth was formed 4.5 billion years ago. Homo sapiens have inhabited this planet for approximately 150,000 years. But it was the Cognitive Revolution (70,000 to 30,000 years ago) that brought about language and information sharing that made humankind such a dominant species. We created permanent settlements for the first time about 45,000 years ago. These settlements were fishing villages. It is here that dogs became the first domesticated animals. After hunter-gatherers came the emergence of farmers and herders and the agricultural revolution. At this point, humankind begins to control the environment for its benefit. Animals are penned, fences go up, and crops are planted.

The fairly recent scientific and industrial revolutions have brought enormous benefits to us all. Education expanded, and communication and travel brought us all closer. We now are living longer due to better medicine and a reduction in violence. Generally, we benefit from more material resources, but there is a cost. And it's a steep one. Consumerism has become a trap that creates continual, unsatisfied needs and shallow solutions to them. Traditional community systems have broken down, leading to more pressured lives, alienation, depression, and addictions. Spiritual needs have become great as institutions falter.

Across the centuries, Western civilization has seen the growth and entrenchment of the belief in a hierarchical order of all creation with humankind at the summit. For example, Aristotle taught that there was a holy ladder with us at the top and the rungs filled with animals, insects, plants, rocks, and so on down. In Genesis, we read that we are created in God's image and rule over all. It is easy to interpret this as human superiority instead of stewardship. Descartes, often referred to as the first modern philosopher, taught that we humans are gifted with innate knowledge making us superior beings. Darwin famously contributed to the theory of evolution, including the survival of the fittest, which reinforced the perception of humans as supreme. This way of viewing the world and our place in it is deeply ingrained in most of us. We may not even be aware of it. It is critical that we grow in understanding and that we see the many implications in our daily lives. We must beware of hubris. It was always punished by the Greek gods, and in the Abrahamic traditions, it turned angels into devils.

What do religions tell us? As they arose across the globe as long as five thousand years ago, religions have been challenged to stay relevant and meaningful. We will see from indigenous peoples and Celts examples of great guidance. But again and again, religious institutions have been damaged and, at times, discredited. This has created millions of unaffiliated spiritual seekers who long for a connection to the eternal. We can understand this crisis of confidence as a clearing out of old ways while still honoring what is most beautiful and valuable. We are also witnessing the origination of entirely new forms of spiritual communities. There is hope, excitement, and opportunity within the darkness of a threatening reality. And if we are to survive, a strong ethos for the welfare of Mother Earth and the cosmos must be central to any religious practice. There are lessons from the past we can mine for ecological wisdom to guide us now. Let's look at two sources next.

LESSONS FROM THE CELTS AND FIRST PEOPLES OF THE AMERICAS

"We should understand well that all things are the work of the Great Spirit. We should know that He is within all things: the trees, the grasses, the rivers, the mountains, and the four-legged animals and all the winged peoples."
—Black Elk

The first peoples of North America lived in harmony with the natural world. They had a deep wisdom that European settlers were not able to grasp. If only they had. If they had listened with open minds, the world would be a different place now. It is not too late. We can still benefit greatly from the traditional core teachings of indigenous peoples. Here are a few of those for reflection. First, to honor the natural world and see the divinity within all, animate and inanimate. Second, to understand that we can learn from the natural world through observation: deep looking and deep listening. The resulting teachings allow us to live in harmony with all and to value that harmony highly. Third, that everyone and everything exists in a web of life, infused with divine mystery. Every being, animal, plant, or mineral has a role, a gift, and a responsibility. Nothing is to be exploited. Nothing is wasted. This stance is fundamentally different from the European conquerors' objectives of claiming and taming the land and its inhabitants. The very idea of ownership was unknown to Native Americans. They believed that as creator, the Great Spirit was the only possible owner. How strange these peoples, European and indigenous, were to one another and how tragic were the results of their meeting.

It is important to note that the Christian tradition of the Europeans did have some similar teachings in its history. Famous holy ones such as St. Francis, Meister Eckhart, and Hildegard of Bingen were known for their love of the earth and their experiences of mystical union with the natural world. They continue to influence and inspire many people across religious traditions, but not nearly enough. We can be enriched through the continued celebration of their voices.

The Celtic Christian church had roots in the earth-based religion led by druids, dating back to at least 5000 BCE. Because Ireland was never invaded by the Romans, it was able to maintain an alternative vision of Christianity which incorporated earlier beliefs. The wisdom of this tradition thrived until its suppression resulting from the Council of Whitby in 664. This council gave authority to the Roman doctrine of duality (secular vs. sacred) rather than the Celtic view that all is sacred. Amazingly, within Ireland and beyond, the Celtic vision has remained vibrant in various ways, often through the creative arts. It is reflected in high crosses, illuminated manuscripts, and the teaching stories and legends of saints, scholars, and other leaders. Among Celtic insights is the importance of all the earth and its creatures, the honoring of the changing seasons, and the recognition of "thin" places where Spirit is most easily accessible. Traditionally, this access to the invisible world is found in thin places such as shorelines, faery forts, groves of trees, circles of standing stones, and at the juncture of two or three streams. For me, the landscape of Ireland offers many doorways to the mystical. This must have been true for the famous Irish teacher of the Celtic church, John Scotus Eriugena (815–877). He taught that there are two ways to know God: through scripture and through creation. His teaching was condemned by the Pope but influenced the Christian mystical tradition taken up by Eckhart, Hildegard, and others. It lives on and has become increasingly salient in our time of a threatened planet.

A TWENTY-FIRST-CENTURY MODEL: THE DONUT

How do we mine the past for the most valuable teachings to guide us in this current era of crisis? We need a major shift in global consciousness, a new socio-economic model. One of the most promising to date was designed by Kate Raworth of the University of Oxford. It is called the Donut Model, and right away, you can see the elimination of hierarchy. The donut is the circle where we want to be. Going beyond the outer ring of the donut places the environment in peril through climate change, lost biodiversity, ocean acidification, chemical pollution, etc. Here we breach our ecological ceiling. In the opposite direction, if we are in the donut hole, we have breached our social foundation. Here humankind's basic needs of health, shelter, food, education, water, etc., are not met. This model is now employed by some cities and has great promise. But what can we do now as individuals? How can we promote better relationships between all members of creation? There is much we can do. There is much that is required.

WHAT IS OUR RESPONSIBILITY?

SEEDS OF CHILDHOOD

Reflecting back in time, many of us find sweet memories of early encounters with nature. When did you first experience awe? Was it a sunset, a butterfly, a first snowfall, a kitten, or the vast ocean dancing on the shore? Such moments of childhood wonder opened mystical doorways. Often, we connect most easily to the Absolute through those same doorways as adults. Many environmentalists, artists, and spiritual masters have special places in their personal history where they experienced transcendence and were forever changed. For Thomas Berry, it was a meadow in South Carolina. For Madeleine L'Engle, it was a starry night sky. For Georgia O'Keeffe, it was the desert of New Mexico. Out of these deep encounters with the Divine came metanoia, a profound change of heart that produced commitments to ethical ideals and fully inhabited lives.

My early encounters with nature were bountiful and nothing less than magnificent. Every summer, my family lived in the Thousand Islands on the St. Lawrence River. We children ran barefoot and free for those charmed months, not a care in the world. Most of my hours were spent alone, which was great training in contemplative living. I was always at ease with solitude and silence, although I learned early that nature is never truly silent. My little dolls were dressed in flowers and had beds of soft, green moss. The earth was closely inspected for miracles of insects, snails, crayfish, shiny stones, and wild strawberries. The back pasture of a neighboring farmer taught me that those cows, so enormous to my little girl self, were shy and gentle. There was no sound except the music of the birds, the howls of the wind, lapping waves, animals' calls, and my humming. There was no technology, no television, no contact with the outside world. This is the place that most formed me and colors how I see this sacred planet.

CHOOSING HOW TO LIVE

As adults, our consciousness evolves, and we come to understand that we are inextricably part of the cosmos. We recognize that we bear responsibility for our planet. We learn what promotes peace and safety for all beings and their homes. This awareness becomes more and more central to our identity, and we make many changes in how we move through our days. The plastic toothbrush becomes bamboo; the big van becomes a hybrid car, and we shun toxins to embrace natural cleaners. All our habits come under scrutiny, including our eating patterns. Steak loses its appeal when we recognize its great cost to our health, animals, farmworkers, the land, water, and air. We may begin to choose more responsibly sourced meats, more local produce, more vegetarian meals, and vegan options. As we make choices that promote environmental well-being, we nourish our own inner peace, and joy arises. It is important to make any small step in the right direction. The steps keep mounting, and the impact of our footprints on the earth becomes gentler.

Once while staying in Plum Village, Thich Nhất Hanh's monastery in France, I received a powerful teaching in the kitchen. My working meditation on this particular day was to slice apples. I was working my way through a great pile of them, mindful and relaxed. A small, elderly nun came and stood beside me. She took the apple cores I had placed aside to discard and carefully relieved them of more flesh. She said not a word. There was no need. The silent lesson is still with me, and although my practice is quite imperfect, I do waste less. Hers was also a pedagogical lesson. Her teaching was without words yet perfect.

For us all, this is a time to create and celebrate positive change, not an opportunity to judge ourselves and others. It is important to educate, exchange ideas, support, and encourage. Good people become passionate about making change, but heavy hands and harsh words do not help us achieve that goal. Be a champion of Mother Earth with a demeanor of compassion, humor, and gentleness.

SOCIAL JUSTICE AND THE PLANET

We do not all move through life in the same manner. We do not all experience Mother Earth in the same or even similar ways. Some of us are born to privilege: privilege of warmth in winter, shelter in storms, nourishing food, adequate health care, opportunities to learn and work.

Many others are born outside this circle of abundance. There are fundamental injustices all around the globe. People are starving, subjected to racism and sexism, living without the most basic medicine, without clean water or electricity, trafficked for sex or slave labor, and victimized by all kinds of violence from war to random shootings. Everyone has their troubles; everyone suffers. But many of us have the luxury of what might be termed "bourgeois suffering," the suffering that comes with a full life. It is truly painful, but on a different scale altogether. Do we have a responsibility to those who suffer great injustice? If we believe that we are all interconnected spiritually, we absolutely do. Even acting only out of self-interest, our greatest security in this increasingly small world is to provide basic human rights and opportunities to all.

This is a big leap for some of us. And what does it have to do with Mother Earth? There is a great imbalance. Consumerism is a way of life that has become exalted around the globe. To one degree or another, most of us have become trapped in it. It is spiritually empty. Look at the literal burden of our possessions in middle-class America. Our stuff suffocates us. It drains our resources, energy, and joy. Storage facilities overflow. There is a flaw in this economic system based on consuming more and more goods and services; one must always want to buy more. Things are designed to attract our attention, to appeal to us. Advertising's job is to sell us any product, often by appearing to satisfy inadequacies created by the ads themselves. So, if we own "x," we will gain in status, sex appeal, vitality, or image. The product is designed to make the sale but not to last. If it lasts too long, demand will decrease. Planned obsolescence keeps business going. This works well when the product is made cheaply, with cheap materials that expire. Services are unnecessarily and/or artificially protracted. Such a production scheme impacts the environment in many ways, such as transportation of goods, damage to forests, air, land usage, waterways, and all kinds of natural resources. How we make things and provide services directly impacts the earth. To do better costs more and reduces profits. Businesses are not inclined to make the hard choices unless the government steps in with regulations. There is always tension between government regulation and the marketplace. At the root of the problem are greed and an unwillingness to consider the long-term environmental impact and the immediate social impact. Of course, there are companies who are making better choices than this scenario offers, and they should earn our loyal patronage. But sadly, they are way too few.

The call to us is for raised consciousness. We must mindfully choose green businesses when purchasing goods and services. We need to reward those who are striving to be environmentally responsible and boycott those who are destructive. If possible, we need to work for companies and organizations that offer us right livelihood.

This includes fair treatment of employees and the earth. Further, we need to educate others and be politically engaged to promote progressive legislation that supports Mother Earth, her laborers, and the coming generations.

ATTITUDE ADJUSTMENTS

How do we motivate ourselves and others to live in a new, socially responsible way? First, we might want to recognize the obstacles. Why are we not making changes more quickly? Looking within ourselves, we can see what is obstructing us and others, for our experiences are common and shared. First, many of us are overwhelmed, at least from time to time, by this issue. It is grave, and we can avoid it rather easily. Distractions are everywhere, and they are constant. There is a lot of support to chuck the whole issue. People feel helpless, hopeless, and resigned to the current situation, even if they understand it well. Second, many are uneducated. They are simply unaware of the gravity of the crisis we are in. This is a failure of education systems, governments, the media, and industrial complex. Third, some are blissfully, overly optimistic Pollyannas taking their cheery route to avoid reality. There will be no magical solution.

Most of us instinctively turn away from what demands change. We are comfortable and do not want that comfort disturbed. But we are standing on a precipice that asks us to have courage and take a risk. The planet will go on. It will thrive. The question is, will homo sapiens? It is possible, but it requires real and widespread change from us all. Across the globe, we must transition to new lifestyles that promise a viable future for generations to come. How do we do this? There are many practical steps you can take, and a checklist to support your change is at the end of this chapter. Spiritually, it is best to tap into our experience of interbeing, our oneness. If we are able to connect to the web of life, we will find the right answers. And these answers will address the needs of all—animals, plants, and minerals, as well as humans. Our experience of life will be centered on deep compassion and a sense of wonder. We become partners in creation and find bounteous ways to support and nurture all that is. This experience of nonduality can be a source of great joy. All that is right in thought, word, and action will stem from this source. Moving in harmony with creation promotes peace within ourselves and makes life truly comfortable, rather than superficially so. This is our hope and the hope of all life on the planet.

BEFRIENDING THE PLANET: AN ACTION CHECKLIST

This is a list of possible action steps you can take to become a devoted caretaker of Mother Earth. Take as many as you can. Take them permanently, or just try them out for a while. Educate yourself on why your actions are important and commit yourself to make a positive change. Add to the list. Do not criticize yourself for what is still left undone. Just keep moving in the direction of healing the planet. Voltaire taught us, "Don't let the perfect be the enemy of the good." Small steps count, and the more small steps, the bigger the count. Pass on the list to others.

TRANSPORTATION

- Take public transportation and support its expansion.
- Drive an energy-efficient car.
- Carpool.
- Organize errands and outings to drive as few miles as possible.
- Bike.
- Walk.
- Take fewer trips, including air travel.
- Use telecommunications for meetings.
- Investigate environmental impact of vacations, including cruise ships.
- Enjoy a car-free day every month, then every week.

FOOD

- Shop local.
- Support good farming practices that protect biodiversity.
- Support food cooperatives and farmers' markets.
- Check food labels.
- Eat plant-based meals as much as possible.
- Invest your time in careful food selection and cooking.

- Buy food with less or no packaging.
- Grow your own food.
- Compost.

HOME ENERGY

- Have an energy audit of your home done.
- Reduce or eliminate air conditioning.
- Reduce heating. Use a programmable thermostat.
- Unplug anything that is not in use.
- Use power strips.
- Air-dry clothes.
- Purchase renewable-source electricity.
- Reduce use of appliances.
- Reduce number of appliances.
- Use solar panels.
- Replace lightbulbs with compact fluorescents.
- Replace paper products with recyclables.
- Use reusable shopping bags.
- Use biodegradable cleaning products.
- Use less hot water.
- Reuse gray water.
- Use rainwater.

LAWNS

- Do not use pesticides or herbicides.
- Consider grass lawn alternatives—rock gardens, vegetable gardens, herb gardens, etc.
- Plant trees.
- Plant native species.
- Pick up neighborhood trash.

REDUCE WASTE

- Buy less. Is "x" really needed? Do I already own something that will do? Can I rent, barter, or borrow?
- Invest in quality goods that do not have to be replaced too soon. Do not support planned obsolescence.
- Share your books and magazines with friends and others, including hospitals, nursing homes, schools, etc.
- Buy second-hand goods.
- Recycle all you can.
- Too much food? Prepare it and freeze or gift.

PROMOTE CHANGE

- Vote for candidates who are committed to protecting the environment, and therefore us.
- Write letters to the editor to support progressive environmental legislation.
- Be active in environmental organizations—local, national, and international.
- Promote these causes on social media.
- Write stories, create art, and do all you can to educate others. Change hearts and minds.
- Meditate regularly to be clear about your intentions and actions.
- Pass on this list.

QUESTIONS FOR REFLECTION

1. When have you stood in awe of creation? Can you connect in that way again?
2. What steps can you take today to do just a little better for Mother Earth?
3. What long-range goals can you work toward for a more balanced world?
4. How can you educate and support others in this revolution?
5. What is your experience of the web of life, and how can you strengthen and sustain that awareness?
6. What spiritual practices center you?

CREATIVE STRETCH

1. If someone is not well mentally, physically, or spiritually, nature is a great source of healing. There are medicinal properties found in herbs that have been passed down since Hildegard of Bingen recorded them in the twelfth century. There are spring waters that people turn to when ill. Mountain air is seen as pure and healing. All the elements can be employed in bringing us into balance. The beauty found in nature is healing when simply gazed upon. It can be as simple as looking up at the night sky, walking in a garden, or enjoying a potted plant. Beauty uplifts our hearts and reminds us of the great mystery of life. It engenders hope. Contemplate nature's healing gifts. How can you employ them in mending your life and the lives of others?
2. This following creative stretch is written as an outdoor activity, but if there are limitations on that possibility it may also be done inside with something as simple as a plant, a goldfish or a flower. If you are doing this as a group be sure to respect each other's privacy and set an end time before you begin.

EXPLORING SPIRIT AND NATURE

- Enter time outdoors with a spirit of openness and curiosity.
- Set an intention for this adventure.
- Maintain silence.
- Engage your senses.
  Look big. Look small.
  Note sounds.
  Be aware of textures. Touch carefully.
  What do you smell? What tastes come to mind?
- Observe.
  Be intuitive.
  Stop and be still.
  What attracts you?
  What qualities/feelings are brought to mind by what attracts you?
  Remain present.
- Journal, draw, photograph, or use whatever means appeal in this moment to enter communion with Mother Earth.

Meditation on the Cosmos

Breathing in, I feel the air enter my body.
Breathing out, I release.
Air entering, releasing.
Air entering, releasing.

Turning inward, I breathe into my heart space.
Touching my center, releasing.
Touching my center, resting.
Releasing, resting.
Releasing, resting.

Behind closed eyes, I enter darkness.
Sheltering darkness, warm darkness.
In the quiet, I float—
ascending on the air surrounding me,
bringing me between worlds.

The vastness of space invites me.
Space within, space without.
The ancient song of the universe sings to me.
Light pours from sunbeams and moonbeams,
soft light, sparkling light, radiant light,
soft light, sparkling light, radiant light.
Here is the peace of solitude.
Here is the peace of solitude
in the midst of teeming creation.
Here is the comfort of pattern—
and the relief of patterns broken,
constellations and shooting stars.

The surprise of color breaks through—
violet, red, yellow, blue, orange, green—

flashes of joy erupting spontaneously,
sparking the dance of imagination.

Floating on the Milky Way,
stars sparkle into eternity.
Timelessness.
Cradled as in a holy mother's arms,
peace within, peace without—
the universe within, the universe without.
Touching transcendence.
Breathing in freedom, breathing out joy. (Bell)
Breathing in freedom, breathing out joy. (Bell)
Breathing in freedom, breathing out joy. (Bell 3x)

CHAPTER SEVEN

GRATITUDE

*"Gratitude is not only the greatest of the
virtues but the parent of all others."*
—Cicero

A mong the first phrases we are taught is "thank you." We remember our parents asking, "What do you say?" as they handed us a toy or a cookie. Those of us with children raised them in the same way. We wanted them to have good manners and get along well in society. Expressions of gratitude are required for social inclusion.

We also know how offended we can become if someone fails to thank us in a timely and sincere manner. This leads us to one of the hot-topic etiquette questions of our time. Is an email thank you adequate, or is a handwritten note required? Regardless of your answer to that weighty query, a failure to express gratitude, and to express it as expected, can seriously damage a relationship. All this points to the importance of gratitude in contemporary American culture, as well as in most other cultures. It is a norm that we live by.

What we must reflect on is whether our good manners are rote or connected to our hearts. Often it is just a reflex, all of us complying with convention without missing a beat. We do a lot of things this way, from brushing our teeth, to kissing a loved one goodbye, to putting on our seatbelts. We would be seriously hamstrung if we had to stop and consider every movement we made through the day. But gratitude is a place where we can benefit from reflection. If our expressions of gratitude connect with both our minds and hearts, they become a spiritual practice. This is a boon for us and everyone around us. Gratitude practice is intentional, thoughtful, and regularly cultivated, ideally on a daily basis. It moves us from pessimism to optimism, from feelings of scarcity to abundance, from restlessness to contentment, from grumpy to joyful, and from sleep-walking through our days to living in awe. Gratitude is a bonanza!

HOW GRATITUDE WORKS

Today, scientific research tells us that a regular practice of gratitude will improve our physical and psychological health, relationships, sleep, and self-esteem. All good reasons to start giving thanks with enthusiasm. When we establish a solid practice of gratitude, our perception of our lives and the world around us changes. Spiritually, we become aware of the great richness we dwell in, no matter our circumstances. There are always reasons to be grateful. Kabir, the fifteenth-century mystic and poet, tells us, "*I laugh when I hear the fish in the sea are thirsty.*" We often restrict ourselves like those fish. We grasp at things and people; we become attached to the fleeting; we long for what is not available. We want to change what cannot be changed, and therefore, we live in misery. When we start to rest our minds on the beauty and bounty of our lives, we shift. This is gratitude at work. We can live in a way that supports this internal movement and brings us increased peace and joy. It all takes place in our minds with no change in external circumstances needed. Through gratitude, we attain contentment, and our hearts are able to open wide.

As our practice of gratitude moves us to a place of abundance, we initiate change in our behavior and relationships. Our minds turn us in a clear direction toward generosity. We want to share our many forms of wealth. This includes the actual giving of material goods and financial gifts. We know we live with many rich, varied resources at our disposal, while others live in need. We can learn to trust that sharing only enriches ourselves, as well as others. It does not impoverish or diminish us. What impoverishes us is believing there will never be enough, that we are in danger in some way. This creates fear, and fear is the opposite of love, our highest spiritual aspiration.

But generosity goes beyond the material. We can learn to become more generous with our time, giving it where it is most beneficial without resentment. We can give gifts of our talents. We all know how to do so many things. You are reading this right now. That is a skill that can be shared with others by reading to the blind, teaching those who are illiterate, or volunteering at a school to tutor children. If you think you don't have talents to share, please pause and reflect on that. You do many things well, and sharing those abilities will benefit you, as well as those you help.

We also can be generous with our thoughts. We can move from a judging mind to an open, curious, accepting mind. We can listen to others deeply without dragging past impressions and experiences into the conversation. We can actively work to change our attitudes in ways that make us more loving in all circumstances. As we do this, we find ourselves moving to another level of consciousness—interbeing.

Interbeing, a term coined by Thich Nhất Hạnh, is the experience of connection to all that is. This truth is part of other traditions too: the web of life of America's First Peoples, the Seventh Principle of Unitarians, Celtic cosmology, and Christianity's Cosmic Christ. Interbeing, the opposite of separation, acknowledges that we live in a world where all is impacted by everything else. This includes all creatures and life forms who share the planet with us. It also includes the elements—fire, earth, water, and air. When we look deeply into our lives, we can see that we are dependent on so many people, material goods, and circumstances. We come to know in a profound way that we are never alone. That is an impossibility. All that we think, do, and say impacts others just as what others are thinking, saying, and doing impacts us. We are intimately connected even when we are physically alone and feel we are separate. That is just an illusion. With spiritual practice, we come to understand that we "inter-are" with our fellow humans and all the rest of the natural world. This indicates a great responsibility to the planet and its inhabitants who sustain our lives. Meditating on interbeing helps us grow in wisdom and compassion for all that is.

As we contemplate interbeing, we are moved to an ever-deepening appreciation of the complex systems of life on our small planet, including our own manifestation. Miracles abound, and we can see them clearly. This leads us to greater gratitude, and we see that cycle spiraling from gratitude to abundance to generosity to interbeing and back again to gratitude. Being aware of this pattern can help us nurture it. There are many ways to strengthen our connection to gratitude.

THE TRUE NATURE OF GENEROSITY

The art of giving requires us to give with an open hand. If we are generous, we do not close our fist, literally or metaphorically, around what we offer to others. Watch for expectations that can start to arise when giving. They seem to want to intrude on the experience. A gift is not an exchange or a trade. It is something entirely different. A gift does not have requirements or conditions attached to it. And a true gift is given freely and let go of in totality. Consider giving anonymously. In this way, we are not asking for the payback of praise, recognition of our better natures, or thanks. We clearly are not asking for any gift in return. Giving anonymously is giving with a totally open hand.

There can be times when giving is not advisable. It may interject us where we do not belong, or it may disempower the receiver. Worst of all, it may give a signal that we do not have faith in the receiver's abilities and strengths. Too much help can become a serious obstacle to growth. It can demoralize and dishearten. That certainly is not the outcome we want. It is always wise to consider carefully if there is a downside to making any offering. If you are not sure, wait until things become clearer.

Your open heart will often have an impulse to give to others in some way. Listen to those impulses, for they are important messengers. Do not act on the impulse, but see it as a call to reflection. Consider your own needs first to be sure you take good care of yourself in a fundamental way. This self-care is good for you and for those around you. Once your own needs are acknowledged and provided for, see if giving the gift is truly wise and helpful and if you have the necessary resources. If so, go ahead, follow your heart and let your loving spirit bless the world!

Gratitude for Suffering

The Guest House
This being human is a guest house.
Every morning a new arrival.
A joy, a depression, a meanness,
some momentary awareness comes
as an unexpected visitor.
Welcome and entertain them all!
Even if they are a crowd of sorrows,
who violently sweep your house
empty of its furniture,
still, treat each guest honorably.
He may be clearing you out
for some new delight.
The dark thought, the shame, the malice.
meet them at the door laughing and invite them in.
Be grateful for whatever comes.
because each has been sent
as a guide from beyond.

This poem by Rumi, the thirteenth-century Sufi mystic, and translated by Coleman Barks, eloquently articulates an important life teaching. We are invited to see all that happens to us, all that crosses our paths, as guests. This requires us to extend hospitality to whatever and whomever life brings us. Opening ourselves to all is a challenging practice. How can we feel good about failed relationships, sickness, the loss of loved ones, and all kinds of misfortunes? We are asked to consider our misfortunes deeply, to not turn away in avoidance or numb ourselves in any way. It seems to take a super-human effort to stay present and look hardship in the eye. We are already suffering, and now we are being advised not to seek comfort by running as fast as we can in another direction. Why?

It is through hardship that we grow in mind and spirit. Critical lessons can be learned through suffering. It may be the best place to learn empathy. If you have been through a difficult divorce, you will never dismiss someone else's pain in similar circumstances. We can read about it, hear about it, see it, but nothing compares with actually going through such an experience. This is one of the reasons support groups are so effective. Those who share suffering of any kind have a unique kinship. If you are fighting a serious illness, your conversation with someone doing the same will offer special gifts that those outside the experience cannot share. Through your own suffering, you will find that you have new gifts to offer, new sources of generosity.

Suffering also gives us the chance to learn what we are made of—strength, resilience, creativity, compassion, and so much more. If we are recovering from the loss of a loved one, we find out that we are survivors, even if we are swallowed up by grief. We learn that deep down, below it all, there is a place of peace and strength that will allow us to move forward. We might not see it right away. But we will find it, like a well in a desert, if we are spiritually active, aware, and patient. Eventually, we discover that we can even touch joy in this relationship once again. We can remain in relationship even without physical presence, and we can take delight in our memories.

Suffering is a doorway to interbeing. We all suffer, and we all have a role in relieving the suffering of others. This is one of the fundamental aspects of life. It is here that we find meaning; we become creative in offering our lives in service. To do so, one does not have to sell everything and go to the poorest of countries to work. There is plenty of good to be done right in our own backyards. Even in affluent neighborhoods, there is often great poverty of spirit. Serve what is in front of you today, and that will be perfect.

OBSTACLES TO GENEROSITY AND GRATITUDE

There are several obstacles to living with generosity and gratitude. The first is our own self-concept. Often, we do not see ourselves as capable of helping or having much to offer. Our lives are so incredibly blessed, and yet we feel impoverished. Thich Nhất Hanh expresses this compellingly in his poem, "Our True Heritage."

You, the richest person on Earth,
who have been going around begging for a living,
stop being the destitute child.
Come back and claim your heritage.
We should enjoy our happiness
and offer it to everyone.
Cherish this very moment.
Let go of the stream of distress
and embrace life fully in your arms.

Investigate your own true self and be honest about all that you have and are capable of offering. Nothing will bring more happiness to your life than loving service to this planet and its inhabitants.

Fear is an efficacious block to our gratitude and generosity. It is the work of the ego and needs to be confronted firmly. Once we practice facing our fears, they start to diminish, and our hearts are able to open. So ask yourself what it is exactly that brings up fear. How does that fear manifest in your life? What is the basis of it, and how can that be debunked? Fears are future oriented. Stay in the present.

Fear is centered on the self. Mistrust is centered on others. Often there are roots in our childhood that make mistrust flourish in us today. If you find it hard to trust others and/or you are cynical, it is good to spend time reflecting on why this is so. There may be some good reasons, but once you understand them, things come into perspective. Mistrust, like fear, robs us of our joy. If needed, work with a spiritual director or therapist to address these energies which impact the quality of our lives.

Ignorance and misinformation sadly abound. They certainly are obstacles to living a life of spiritual depth. Carefully consider the sources of information that you let into your days. These include computers, phones, television, newspapers, magazines, movies, and all the people who are in your life. We do not have to, and shouldn't, agree with everything we are exposed to. It is good to listen to all points of view on issues. However, it is not helpful to let sources of division, separation, fear, mistrust, prejudice, and intolerance into our days. These distract us and are insidious in their negative effects on our thinking and our lives.

Consumerism and all the messaging that comes with it lead us to persistent feelings of scarcity, insufficiency, inadequacy, and general discontent. It turns us into hungry ghosts. These impoverished beings in Buddhist teachings endure insatiable hunger. Their empty bellies are swollen, and their tiny mouths and needle-thin long necks make the pathway to satiety impossible. In today's society, it is easy to become these miserable creatures. Always longing. Never content. We must carefully guard our well-being in the face of the siren call of advertising. It is powerful, and it is everywhere. You might like to take just a single day and note all the times you hear, see, smell, taste, and touch the tempters of the marketplace. It is a good practice to note needs versus wants and what is sufficient. Our gratitude comes from a place of plenty, not from always wanting the next, newest, brightest, shiniest thing. We can hardly feel generous if we are always focused on seeking more for ourselves. This manner of turning inward creates the consumers the marketplace desires, but it does not create generous, loving people. Every day, we can check in with ourselves to look for evidence of a strengthening, selfish ego. Have we been self-centered, jealous, stingy, or covetous? Just be curious and move toward your original, good, and generous nature.

GRATITUDE PRACTICES

How can we strengthen our experience of gratitude? If you meditate or pray at the start of the day, as I hope you do, that is a great time to say thank you. Acknowledge a few things that you are especially grateful for each morning. Remember someone who has been helpful at this time of your life. As you move into your day, call to mind the little things that bring you beauty and joy. It is good to be grateful for the flowers on the table, the coffee you are savoring, or the good book in your hand. It is a practice. You can simply acknowledge with your awareness, or you can say a quiet *thank you*. How you do this does not matter as long as you create the shift within your heart.

Gratitude journals are popular now, and there are lovely ones published for you to utilize as a practice. However, you can just take any old notebook and start making daily or weekly gratitude lists. You might like to make two lists: one for big items and one for small. The big things are easy to recognize. Special events such as graduations, weddings, or holidays fill us with gratitude. Occasionally we may feel grateful to get a clean bill of health or conquer a dicey problem. And every day, we can be grateful to those who came before us, the ancestors of blood, spirit, and land who paved our way. We can bow before nature and greet each dawn as the extraordinary gift it is. In addition, we can look for all manner of small things to be grateful for and become even more expansive in this practice. So, when the weather is horrid, and you sit in front of a warm fire, don't just note how pleasant it is; say *thank you*. You'll find there are hundreds of times a day you can invite those words into your mind. Their impact is cumulative and elevating.

Another idea is to utilize a gratitude jar. I have a lovely one made by a potter that was given to me by my cousin Nan and her husband George. Each time I use it, I think of them and am grateful for their presence in my life. The jar works like a journal. I keep little slips of paper next to it and write down a cause of gratitude each day, slipping it into the jar. After a couple of months, I pour them all out on the table and read through the pile. It is a great reminder of the richness of my life. Then I start anew. You can make your own jar by decorating any ordinary one you have on hand, or you can find one to purchase. Also, think about giving one as a meaningful gift to encourage someone else's gratitude practice.

An interesting idea you can try is putting your senses to use as avenues to gratitude. At any time, just pause and think of each of the five senses: hearing, sight, smell, touch, and taste. Name something you are grateful for that you receive through each sense. You can do this briefly or at length. Be sure to be thankful for the senses themselves and all the people and material goods that keep them working for you at an optimum level.

Try employing the words *thank you* or *gratitude* as a mantra. Repeat them over and over again as you walk, use prayer beads, or just sit quietly. This is a powerful practice that does not require an object for your gratitude unless you wish to incorporate one. It is an opening of the heart done with intention and fidelity.

Write thank-you notes. Whether you choose to write them online or on stationary, saying thank you in writing is important. That's why we were taught to do so when we were young. After opening Christmas gifts, my siblings and I were not supposed to play with it, eat it, read it, watch it, or do anything with a present until the thank you was written. There was also a three-day deadline. On the third day, the note had to be in the mail. I still prefer getting a card or letter in the mail. There is an intentionality to receiving someone's thoughts, carefully handwritten, put in an envelope, and then mailed. It is profoundly generous and kind to take it a step further and write a letter to someone in your past who impacted your life in a significant manner. Take the time to recall just how they made a difference for you and tell them how it felt then and why it remains important now. Everyone likes to be appreciated, and just because we are grateful doesn't mean that the gratitude is known and received. Telling someone they were instrumental to your growth is a life-affirming gift. It is in your power to give it.

QUESTIONS FOR REFLECTION

1. Where do you give your time, talent and money? Do you put these sources of your precious energy into efforts aligned with your values?
2. Recall remarkable acts of generosity that have blessed your life. Have you expressed gratitude? Would you like to do so again?
3. What book had the greatest impact on your life? Who can you give it to? This could apply to movies, music, etc.

CREATIVE STRETCH

1. Create something with your hands and heart to offer a special thank you.
2. Your body brings you many gifts each day. How can you express gratitude to your body? What gift can you give it?
3. Keep a gratitude journal. Utilize art, words, or both.
4. Take photographs of things you are grateful for and collect them into an album or collage.

Gratitude Meditation

Begin by centering on your breath.

In, out.
Deep, slow.
Calm, ease.
Smile, release.

Empty your mind of all concerns.
Now drop your awareness down to your heart space.

Breathing in blessings. Breathing out gratitude.
Bring into awareness all the little moments of beauty in this day.

- the first sip of tea or coffee, the warmth it brings
- the lightening sky
- a bit of music, birdsong
- a flower, a tree
- someone's smile, laughter

What small moments have you experienced today that nourished your heart?
Let gratitude grow within.
Breathing in blessings. Breathing out gratitude. (Bell 3x)

Now, open your awareness to the most significant gifts you've received.

- the circumstances of time and place that good fortune brought you
- the relationships that have shaped you
- the teachings you have been blessed to receive
- the suffering that has enlarged your understanding and heart

• the health of body, mind, and Spirit that sustains you

Let gratitude grow within.
Breathing in blessings. Breathing out gratitude. (Bell 3x)

Gratitude growing, large and small—
Swelling, multiplying, nourishing.

Gratitude blooming into generosity,
Endless generosity of heart,
Endless generosity of word,
Endless generosity of thought,
Endless generosity of action,
Endless generosity of being.

Blessings, the unending source of gratitude (bell),
Gratitude, the wellspring of generosity (bell),
Generosity, overflowing into joy. (Bell 3x)

CHAPTER EIGHT

EMBODIED SPIRIT

"The Word is living, being, spirit, all verdant greening, all creativity. This Word manifests itself in every creature."
—*Hildegard of Bingen*

As a spiritual director, I spend a lot of time talking with people one-to-one about the things that are closest to their hearts. It is a great privilege to listen as they share their lives, including their histories, fears, and aspirations. These are not ordinary conversations. They go deep into the territory of faith, doubt, suffering, and hope. Many times, the body comes up. This is not unexpected because we are our bodies; we cannot exist without our physical manifestations. But still, I am surprised at how often body issues arise. It seems that we do not pay enough attention to how our bodies and spirits connect. The physical body is a multi-disciplinary, multi-cultural field of inquiry. Let's look at where we are coming from and how we wish to go forward.

When we were born, we were born into a particular time, race, gender, culture, and place. We were born with innate strengths and weaknesses. We were born into a family with a religious tradition, or more than one, or none. Take a moment to consider all that. The possibilities of birth are endless, but we were all created unique individuals with various resulting consequences. How, when, and where we were born have a great impact on who we are, including our bodies. A woman's experience is different from a man's. A black man's experience is different from a white man's. A Muslim child grows up with different customs than a Buddhist child. A blind child experiences youth differently than a sighted one. Endless variables such as these have physical implications.

Our ancestors live on in us. We may have our grandfather's temper or our great-aunt's eyes. We are linked to all beings, but our links to our biological line are empirically clear and often easy to see or feel. It is up to us to maximize the good qualities that have been handed down to us and minimize the challenging ones. In a similar manner, we all are children of cultures that have shaped us and everyone around us. We have inherited incredibly rich traditions that have brought much goodness and beauty to the world. But we have also inherited some disturbing beliefs and practices, some deeply embedded prejudices. It is our task to weed out the troublesome, divisive teachings and to help move the world forward in a more enlightened direction.

Racial discrimination has been a part of the world for as long as history has been recorded. Because race is physically manifested, it is an easy way to demark one against another. For some unknown reason, lighter skin has been deemed superior to darker. It could have been the reverse. This phenomenon is true around the world, in African and Asian cultures as well as Western. It is a false distinction, obviously. Levels of melanin determine skin color, and it is truly only skin deep. Yet horrors have been and continue to be inflicted on people designated by some as racially inferior. We all know this, and our crucial challenge is to find ways to move us out of this misguided tragedy. If you think you are not prejudiced, think again. The culture around you is powerful, and it impacts us all. Religions are not immune, sadly. Although religions point us to the highest levels of human aspiration and development, they often fail. And they have failed here. Is your religious community welcoming to all races? Does it reach out? Is your religious community using its beliefs as support for discrimination? If you create a culture of exclusivity, some people become outgroups. Everyone should be alert to teachings that divide rather than unite. No values should be elevated higher than compassion and love.

We have a similar, difficult inheritance regarding gender. In ancient times, it must have seemed strange to everyone that women were able to give birth. Certainly the biology of conception was not known, and women must have been regarded with awe as they produced the progeny that allowed the human race to continue. Besides awe, we can believe that the implied feminine power of fertility was feared by men. This fear and awe were complicated by the fact that men were physically stronger, and in this way, women were seen as lesser humans. Women were tied to the home as men went off to hunt and gather, and later as they worked the fields. So, the roots of patriarchy were planted and have grown through the ages. There are inspiring exceptions to this narrative, histories of strong women, goddesses, and rare groups where women had real power. But patriarchy is a stumbling block for most that still needs to be addressed.

Patriarchy has long been thought to benefit men, and in some ways, that has been historically true. However, when we think of the potential for human development and the promise of what that can be, we realize that patriarchy is a system that puts everyone at a disadvantage. Men and women should be allowed to grow, learn, and shape their lives as best suits their talents and inclinations. They should have the freedom to become all they can be. That means that some men might well wish to be homemakers, to teach young children, and to nurse, and some women may flourish as warriors, chief executive officers, or priests. Recognizing everyone's rights, men and women, to become the people they were born to be extends naturally to those identifying as LGBTQ, agender, or asexual. We can see that gender is quite fluid if we pause and look around at the people we know and love. We must support, with great compassion, the journey each individual is on in matters of self-identity.

Another area of concern that is rooted in the body is its vulnerability. At times we experience illness and become weakened by it. We often need the help of professionals and others who are close to us. Some of us were born disabled or become disabled through accident or aging. Those disabilities may manifest in physical or mental difficulties. Again, we may find we need assistance. All of us know the vulnerability of childhood when we were small and much weaker than adults. The horrors that are perpetrated against children still are with us: trafficking, abuse, sexual assault, child labor, and more. Another time of vulnerability occurs near the end of our lifespan if we are fortunate enough to live many years. We become older adults who are physically weakened and, at times, mentally weakened. Again, there are many who are not well protected and become victims of various forms of abuse. We must do what we can to prepare for this stage of life and our own protection. As community members, we must be active in offering support to those who are in this state of vulnerability.

In the United States, we are challenged to bring the values we hold most high to implement change in particularly troubling realities. Some of these are connected to our physical bodies, such as the prevalence of guns in society, racism, religious intolerance, homelessness, the many manifestations of our environmental crisis, hate crimes, domestic violence, many forms of discrimination, and poverty. If we are a loving people who value each human life, we have an obligation to act in ways that move us forward toward a more balanced and compassionate society. We have stumbled often, but we need to maintain hope and a commitment to a just, free, and secure society that contributes to the well-being of this increasingly small planet.

CONNECTIONS

One cannot really separate the body from the human experience of mind and spirit. They are inextricably linked to one another and make up a dynamic whole that is ever-evolving. Historically there were many who tried to separate these aspects of our humanity and even to label one as good (spirit or mind) and the other as bad (body). This dichotomy flows from ancient Greek thought and is perpetuated by Descartes, St. Paul, Augustine, and others. It became a widespread cultural belief that the sacred and profane correlate with the spiritual and physical aspects of humanity. We are now evolving from that duality into a more sophisticated understanding of the interconnection within each being, as well as among all beings. My personal belief is that the spark of divinity is within each particle of creation. It can be corrupted and distorted through life events, but it remains at the heart of all.

If you are still wondering what the body has to do with spirituality, here are just some of the ways that religion has utilized the body to express beliefs and promote community: communion, circumcision, dance, self-flagellation, celibacy, yoga, genital mutilation, kneeling, walking meditation, fasting and dietary restrictions, singing, chanting, and anointing. The body is how we receive and share all teachings utilizing our senses of hearing, speaking, touching, smelling, and tasting. These are powerful doorways. How we use them and protect them is critical to our well-being. So let us take a look at how to care for our bodies, and therefore our minds and spirits.

SELF-CARE

Take a moment and come into awareness of your physical being. Close your eyes and see if you can touch the wonder of your body. It is a miracle walking. You are comprised of the four elements: water, fire, earth, and air. These are the same elements that make up all of creation and are testimony to the fact that you are at one with all that is. Somehow, we drift away from this understanding of our own essence. We come to live in our heads and distance ourselves from our earthly nature. We are of the earth just as we are of the heavens. We are glorious expressions of the Divine imagination. Think of that as you sit with your body.

This invitation to self-contemplation and self-care is not selfish. It is easy to feel that we are spending too much time on ourselves. But the reality is most people spend too little. We tend to take care of others before we take care of our own needs. This weakens us and leaves us with less to offer. There is great wisdom in understanding what is required to maximize our potential and then meeting those needs. When finances are involved, you may think it is too expensive.

But if you strengthen yourself now, there will be fewer costs due to physical problems later. Invest in yourself. Remember that you are not separate. Taking care of yourself is foundational to caring for your family and community.

As James Joyce said of Mr. Duffy in *Dubliners*, "*He lived a little distance from his body.*" The quickest correction of that situation, for Mr. Duffy and for us all, is to turn to our breath. The breath is the direct connection of our physical being with the world outside us. It is the taking in of air that sustains us. So, when we feel disconnected from the body, the best thing to do is stop and breathe. The yogis understood this thousands of years ago, and it is still the ideal tool for coming into physical awareness. As we enter this awareness, we can assess how we are. Our body is the best physician we can consult. Truly paying attention to our sensations and feelings will give us a sound assessment. A harmonious body is quiet, but when there is an illness or injury that needs addressing, the body will speak to us. If we refuse to pay attention, the messages will get louder and louder. First, we must take time to stop and listen. Coming into stillness in prayer and meditation is foundational to your mental, physical, and spiritual health. The body scan is a meditation practice that can be helpful. A version of this, in the form of a blessing, is found at the end of the chapter.

Just as our bodies need quiet, they also long for movement. They are designed to move. If we listen to our inner voice, we will hear the call to rise and come out of stillness. We belong to a culture of sitting. We sit at computers, in cars, and in front of TVs. We sit at meals, at ballgames, at movies, and in temples. Our bodies long to dance, run, jump, stroll, skate, ski, play ball, bike, and swing through sun salutations. There is an increasingly popular saying originating from the medical community that sitting is the new smoking. It is not good for our bodies to be too sedentary, nor is it good for our mental health. Movement stimulates chemicals that produce feelings of well-being and even elation. You may feel you don't have time. Be creative. Take your meetings or calls on a walk. You may feel you are unable. Reconsider that and move in the smallest, safest ways you can. It all counts. If needed, get professional support through physical therapy, yoga, a personal trainer, or your physician. Be sure to move in some manner each and every day. You'll be glad you made that commitment.

THE SENSES

The senses are our bridges to the human experience of the world. They enable us to connect through our abilities to see, hear, taste, touch, and smell. They help us understand and interpret what we encounter. They enhance our joy and alert us to danger. If one of our senses is damaged or lost, the others step up to help fill the void. My own family has a blind dog, and although Bodhi has lost his sight, he navigates well. If nothing in his environment is moved, he can get along fine, using his body to gently touch familiar objects he remembers. He often smells his location and always his food. He also compensates by sitting in ways that allow him to physically touch one of us. Although blind, Bodhi has created a secure and loving life through his remaining senses.

Our eyes bring so much information to us. When we look at a person's body language or facial expressions, we often understand far more than his or her words convey. Danger can be recognized instantly when we see a car coming toward us or a lightning bolt in the sky. We also can experience a sense of reverence when we look at nature's beauty, a work of art, a newborn, or the dying. Beauty is everywhere if we train ourselves to look deeply and observe it. And through this opening to beauty, we are elevated and healed.

The ability to smell is powerful. It tells us when something is burning and alerts us to some illnesses. We associate the smell of certain flowers with important times in our lives—times of falling in love, celebration, and death. Think about your memories. Do any of them have odors attached? Perhaps you can bring to mind campfires, favorite foods, a certain perfume, or the ocean. Odors create strong connections. My father smoked cigars, and whenever I smell one, he is instantly in my mind and heart, even though he has been dead nearly forty years.

Our hearing also brings us critical input as we hear alarms, cries of pain, or shouts of jubilation. When we listen deeply, we hear more than the words that are being shared; we hear the tones and the context that carry those words. We can often understand the intentions behind them and the complexity of their origins. We hear hesitancies and the silences between words. If our practice is to listen without judgment, we can truly hear. Beyond words, we can receive the great gift of music through our hearing. Music can help us connect to divinity by offering a pathway to transcendence. How often have you been transported when listening to great music? Have you experienced chanting? You can receive benefits through listening, or even better, through chanting yourself. It is meditation joined to the rhythms and tones of music. Remember that hearing is the last of our senses to leave us. If someone is gravely ill or dying, always assume that he/she can hear you. Guard your words carefully and use them to comfort and uplift.

Touch is critical to our physical well-being. We all know that babies can fail to thrive if they are not held often by caring adults. In fact, we can all fail to thrive at any point in life if touch is denied us. This tactile connection might be the greatest gift of massage therapy. This practice is nearly five thousand years old, and it is called therapy for a good reason. It offers caring touch and an opportunity to turn within and connect deeply with our own physical reality at that moment in time.

When considering touch, we enter the realm of our sexuality. Sex is necessary for the propagation of humanity. It is essentially good and can express great love and joy, as well as produce offspring. Our sexuality has also been the source of great suffering. It all depends on how we employ the potential within our bodies. Here we can see the connection between mental intention and physical expression. Our sexuality can be used to express love, for mutual or selfish pleasure, or tragically as an instrument of violence.

While on this important topic, let us consider abortion. Good people differ in their positions, and we all need to listen to one another with openness. It is unfortunate that this has become such a political controversy in the United States. It is certainly a spiritual concern and a medical issue. Life begins at different points in various traditions: at conception is the most common theory, but also at forty days, when the fetus is viable on its own or with the first breath. Medical issues are complicated but real, including the health of the mother and unviable fetuses. It seems that we want to make a nuanced and complicated matter simple. This is not a topic that can be reduced to slogans. Those of us who are old enough remember when abortions were illegal and the horrors that were common. Abortion is not desired by anyone. It is always tragic and emotionally painful. One way we can reduce the number of abortions is to provide comprehensive health care for all women and men so that unwanted pregnancies do not occur so frequently. Spiritual direction is needed as women, and often their partners, navigate these bodily experiences. All need to be held in compassion and love. All need to be free of fear.

Taste is the last sense for us to consider. When we were young, we held out our tongues and explored the world. We tasted snowflakes, salt water, and bugs that flew in our mouths. We were always tasting. As we got older, we learned to limit our tasting to our meals. Food is necessary for the health of our bodies and for our very survival. But what we eat has large implications for the planet and its animals, as well as for ourselves. So here are some questions to ask yourself:

- What food nourishes my body, mind, and spirit, promoting peace and happiness within me?
- Where did this food come from, and how far did it have to travel to reach me?
- How much packaging was used?
- How much land and water were used to produce this food?
- Was there waste that impacted the environment negatively?
- Were chemicals utilized in production of this food that are harmful to me, other consumers, animals, the environment, and farmworkers?
- Does cultivation and slaughter of this food impact farmworkers in any negative way?

- Do I eat moderately, taking what I need and maintaining aware-ness of the hungry?
- How are other living beings impacted by my choices?
- How are future generations impacted by my choices?
- Do I eat with mindfulness and gratitude?
- Do I waste food?
- Do I utilize food to connect to others by showing kindness, joy, compassion, friendship, and love?

LONELINESS

The former US Surgeon General Vivek Murthy said, "*During my years caring for patients, the most common pathology I saw was not heart disease or diabetes; it was loneliness.*" Although loneliness is not a diagnosable illness, it is now a worldwide epidemic. Affecting the more affluent nations, the reasons are many: increased rates of divorce, lower rates of childbirth, high rates of job mobility, lack of workplace and religious communities, and declining meaningful social connections. Most recently, all around the world, we have experienced increased isolation and resulting loneliness due to the pandemic of COVID-19. The costs are not fully known yet, but they are many and long-term.

Why does this matter to our physical bodies? There is a clear con-nection. Loneliness causes stress, and stress often causes high blood pressure, weakened immune systems, increased inflammation, and more. Isolation also leads to unhealthy habits, which then promote ill-health. A Brigham Young University study revealed that loneli-ness shortens life by fifteen years. Since nearly half of all Americans today say they are lonely, we are talking about a serious trend in public health. The statistics from many research studies are stag-gering. For example, between 1985 and 2009, the average American's social network decreased by more than one-third. Eight million US citizens are without close family members. In Japan, more than half a million people spent at least six months at home with no outside contact. Forty-one percent of the British say a pet or television is their main source of company. And one finding that surprised me was that young people are most at risk of being lonely.

What can we do about this challenge? You can be alone and yet not experience persistent loneliness. You can be in constant contact with people and feel totally cut-off and isolated. What seems to be missing for so many of us is quality relationships where one feels understood and accepted. It takes time to build significant relationships, and with high mobility rates, it becomes quite difficult to begin again and again or to try to sustain relationships over distances. Perhaps a good place to start is to be aware of the problem within our social circles. If we suspect that someone might be lonely, we can ask them. If we are sure, then we can take time to reach out or to help them connect to resources in our communities. Our retreat centers, churches, temples, synagogues, mosques, and other religious organizations traditionally have a high moral responsibility for hospitality. We are brothers and sisters who need to share meaningful experiences, and where better than in spiritual settings? For the good of us all, let's take this epidemic of pain seriously.

LOSS

There is another public health issue that impacts all of us in the United States. Our love affair with guns and violence in its many forms is part of our heritage. We were founded through the perpetration of genocide on the native peoples of North America, and we cultivated gunslinging heroes for generations. We now face the dark side of this heritage and its resultant destruction. We want to carry guns to protect our freedom. But if our young people are living in fear of being shot in their classrooms, what kind of freedom is that? We must address this issue before we have become completely inured to regular public killings. Each child or adult struck down is potentially our own beloved one. No less than that. We need to truly care and take steps toward sanity. No other nation on earth has created such a man-made disaster. As I write this, the daily average for people shot in the US is 342, and of that number, ninety-six will die. Today. Many more will grieve for them. In 2018, nearly forty thousand citizens died in this manner. We can do something about these losses.

We also lose many others to drug and alcohol addictions and other mental illnesses. Suicide is connected to firearm and loneliness issues. All of these heartbreaking public concerns are interwoven, and they need our vigilance. We do not have to look far. If you have a family that has not been touched by mental illness, you are the exception. Find ways to contribute to the solution. Break the bonds of shame and share your story; listen to others as they tell theirs. We can work together to build a more empathetic and supportive world. We can heal.

As we age, we experience many losses. We lose loved ones, careers, and homes. Physically we can expect creaky joints, sluggish memories, and diminished eyesight and hearing. Losses can also include more threatening experiences of disease, accidents, and disabilities. Losses come at an increasing rate of speed, and we can feel like our bodies are out of control. It reminds me of adolescence when every day our bodies seemed to reveal something new. Now, as we age, they are starting to weaken and provide us with mini-deaths. Loss in maturity is a spiritual wake-up call, a series of alarm bells, some louder than others. We are going to die, and it is fortunate if we have time to prepare.

DEATH

As we prepare to leave this body, there are some things we may wish to consider. It is necessary to get our affairs in order, including our physical belongings, our wills, our advanced directives, and any other recommended paperwork. There are attorneys who specialize in elder law and are familiar with the law and regulations you need to know about. And despite the title "elder" law, this preparation is not just for the over-seventy age group. If you have any dependents, it is especially important to prepare in this manner.

It is also advisable to talk with a trusted loved one about what you would like to see happen at the time of your death. This includes the time of illness and the actual passing, as well as funeral arrangements. Who would you like at your bedside? Who would you prefer not to be there? Would you like to hear certain music? Is there an image you would like to rest your gaze upon? There is no right or wrong to these requests. It is your time to organize so you can transition in a peaceful manner without any friction, regrets, or unnecessary pain.

And last of all, be sure to consult with a spiritual advisor who can answer your questions, pray with you, negotiate arrangements on your behalf, or simply sit by your side. If you wish to have a wake, a funeral, visiting hours, a cremation, a graveside service, a memorial, a celebration of your life, or any other remembrance, discuss the possibilities. Then you can let it all go. All that has come before will now recede into the distance as you prepare to leave your physical body and enter the light.

CONCLUSION

The body is an enormous field of opportunity for spiritual practice. It provides us with an ever-changing canvas we can learn from as we fully engage. Let us take time to consider our many physical gifts each day and be grateful. Let us rise to the challenges that are presented in this form. And let us understand that our own eternal spirit is surrounding our bodies and minds at all times in loving protection.

QUESTIONS FOR REFLECTION

1. What were the circumstances of your birth? This includes time, place, gender, race, religion, culture, family, and much more. How do you feel about them?
2. Have you ever experienced racism, sexism, or any other form of discrimination? How did you feel at the time? Did you address the problem in any way? What did you learn? How do you feel about it now? Is healing complete?
3. What steps are you taking to make society more just and compassionate? Consider all the organizations you belong to, including family, religious groups, workplace, clubs, and country.
4. How do you care for your own body? Do you need to improve this?
5. How does your body help you evolve spiritually? Take a moment to be grateful.

CREATIVE STRETCH

1. Think about how you loved to move your body when you were a child. What activities did you enjoy? Can you enjoy them—or some variation of them—once again?
2. Consider those who have harmed you in some physical manner. Are you able to forgive them? If not, consider speaking to a spiritual director or counselor about your experience.
3. Go to a dance performance or a sporting event and marvel at the abilities of the human body.
4. Cook something that is healthy for you and the planet. Share it with love.
5. Contribute to those in physical need: the hungry, the homeless, refugees, the lonely, the sick, the blind, or disabled. Can you give of your time as well as your financial resources?
6. Take several magazines and look at all the images. How is the body portrayed? Make a mandala collage of your own body experience using those images and photographs. What does the mandala reveal?

A Self-blessing

This blessing may be edited to reflect your own life experience. Make the blessing your own. If you feel inclined, you may anoint your body with essential oils as you contemplate its wondrous terrain. This blessing may be done standing, sitting, or lying down.

I bless my feet and send gratitude for all the miles walked, from my first step until today. I celebrate you. Thank you for strapping on roller skates, skis, sneakers, and all kinds of fancy footgear. Thank you for raising me up in jumps of joy and for running to safety when fear struck. Thank you for tiptoes, confident strides, and loud stomps.

I bless you, my legs, and send gratitude for all the holding up you have done for so long. Thank you for the grace of ballet and the strength of lifts. Thank you for the long muscles and delicate knees. Thank you for carrying me.

I bless my genitalia of delight and of pain. I bless the birthing center of me. Home of children—longed for, born, miscarried, aborted. Home of the creative impulse, imagination, and dream. Like the Sheela-na-gigs of old, let me display my creativity, call it forth, and bless this world in every way within my reach.

I bless my heart. May it never close before anyone or anything. I celebrate every expression of love that has come to me and gone out from me. May the great generative strength of a compassionate heart be mine, and may it connect me to all that is.

I bless my hands. Busy hands, resting hands, strong hands, arthritic hands, beautiful hands, aging hands. May they always find ways to extend in love through everyday tasks—praying, cooking, making music, turning pages, cleaning, clapping, dressing, writing, healing, magical hands!

I bless my arms—reaching, waving, hugging, swinging, expressive arms.

I bless my mouth. May it speak in kindness always. May it know when to keep silent. May it take in nourishment that is compassionate to me and the planet. May it sing with joy today.

I bless my nose as it smells all the beauty of the earth, the oceans, delicious cooking, flowers, loved ones.

I bless my eyes and invite them to look on all that appears with lovingkindness, always assuming the good. May they see beauty everywhere, even in the most unexpected places. May they know how to look deeply—and not just see.

I bless my ears that they may listen with openness to others. May they regularly receive music and the poetry of the written word, uplifting my heart and spirit.

I bless my mind. May it hold wisdom and peace. May it remain strong with age, and may it bring its gifts to myself and others. May it always serve the greatest good as I grow in understanding.

My heart swells with gratitude for all these changing, dynamic gifts of my physical life. May they be treasured by me each day and utilized in the service of Spirit.

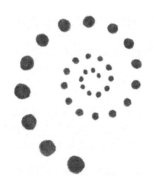

CHAPTER NINE

JOY

"Folks are usually about as happy as they
make up their minds to be."
—*Attributed to Abraham Lincoln*

When conducting a wedding service, I often include this compelling quote in my message to the couple: *"Folks are usually about as happy as they make up their minds to be."* These words hold an empowering belief that can alter our experience of life individually and through our relationships. Abraham Lincoln suffered from depression and lived a life full of inordinate challenges, so he must have contemplated what it meant to be happy, as well as what depression meant. He is telling us that we have some power over our well-being. We can make choices about how we feel, as well as about how we think. The ability to choose joy is life-changing.

But before we go further, let's define the words "happiness" and "joy." The interpretations can be different in various spiritual traditions, so it is helpful to be clear as we begin. For our purposes, happiness is the transient experience of elevated moods and a general sense of well-being. It is when we enjoy laughter and good times. Joy, on the other hand, is a deeper, enduring encounter with spirit. It is profoundly life-giving. Joy can be held in our hearts even in times of deep sorrow and suffering. It is a reflection of coming into wholeness, into our true selves.

JOY ACROSS TRADITIONS

There is a universal acknowledgment of the centrality of joy in spiritual life. We can find many teachings from worldwide sources of wisdom that have endured the test of centuries. Below are a few for you to consider. They are not exclusive to each wisdom tradition, but they are examples of the scope and variety of religious teachings on joy.

Hinduism: Lifelong Joy

The Vedas offer a philosophy that promises the seeker spiritual joy. It sees joy as the logical result of good actions. Among the guidelines are to be kind to strangers, generous to family, friendly with the faithful, respectful of scholars, humble with the elderly, and lovingly strict with one's children. The powerful ideal of ahimsa, or avoiding harm, leads one to be kind not only to strangers and family but to all beings.

In Hinduism, as in other traditions, there are several kinds of joy. The three types distinguished in this religion are physical, mental, and spiritual. One of the interesting insights is that the types of joy change as we move through the stages of life. They become increasingly elevated experiences as a consequence of one's inner growth. The four stages of life are student, householder, old age, and renunciate. So, a Hindu is likely to find happiness in early life through learning and taking on the responsibilities of marriage and family. Later as these pursuits are left behind, he or she is able to pursue liberation and union with the Supreme Self, the ultimate joy.

It is important to note that peace and joy are accessible for the Hindu at all stages of life through devotion. In the words of Paramahamsa Yogananda:

From joy I came,
for joy I live,
and in Thy sacred joy
I shall melt again.

Buddhism: Joy Instructions

The ancient sutras of Buddhism include the Sutra on Happiness (joy). This sutra instructs listeners to do the following: to keep company with wise people, to live in a good environment, to learn and grow, to practice loving speech, to cherish family, to have a vocation that brings joy, to be honest and generous, to be humble, grateful, and polite, to be content with a simple life, and to study scripture and be in contact with monastics. Each element of this formula is practiced as a pathway to a joyful life. The sutra ends with these beautiful words:

To live in the world
with your heart undisturbed by the world,
with all sorrows ended, dwelling in peace—
this is the greatest happiness.
For the one who accomplishes this
is unvanquished wherever she goes;
always he is safe and happy—
happiness lives within oneself.

Judaism: Praise and Joy

Some of the most beautiful words written on joy come from the psalms of Hebrew scripture:

You turned my wailing into dancing;
you removed my sackcloth and clothed me with joy,
that my heart may sing your praises and not be silent,
Lord my God, I will praise you forever.
—Psalm 30:10–13

Here we find not only poetry to feed our soul, but the critical teaching that joy may be found in praise. We do not talk about praise often, but it is a reliable, straight pathway to joy. Think of any moment when your heart has been so moved that you felt the elation of praise spring up within you. It could be as significant as the first time you held your child in your arms or as ordinary as spotting a flash of a bright flower on a rainy day. These invitations are with us always. Our worlds burst with the extraordinary so often that we have become inured to it over the years. Spend a little time with children and latch on to their wonder. When that wonder and awe lift our hearts in praise to the Divine, we experience spiritual joy. It is inevitable. This energy flows in the opposite direction also. If you actively cultivate a practice of praise, you can begin to see the beauty within creation that you may have been missing. The more you see, the greater your joy. Perhaps you might start your mornings with another line from the psalms.

> This is the day the Lord has made, let us rejoice and be glad.
> —Psalm 118:24

Christianity: Love and Joy

> *"Dear Child of God, you are loved with a love that nothing can shake, a love that loved you long before you were created, a love that will be there long after everything has disappeared. You are precious, with a preciousness that is totally quite immeasurable. And God wants you to be like God. Filled with life and goodness and laughter—and joy."*

This blessing from Archbishop Desmond Tutu points to the connection between love and joy. Love is the supreme commandment of Christianity: to love God with all one's heart and to love one's neighbor as oneself. If anyone, of any tradition, experiences the love of the Divine, he or she cannot help but be joyful. This joy remains through all of life's experiences, no matter how difficult. This is most certainly the basis for Pierre Teilhard de Chardin's claim that joy is the infallible sign of the presence of God. In all spiritual settings, we should look for this presence of joy as a sign of elevated conscious-ness and its resultant wisdom.

Islam: Joy and Self-Compassion

When teaching on joy, Islam offers themes of knowledge, enlighten-ment, balance, peace, and tranquility. When one reaches the ideal of achieving these states through submission to God, one is in a state of true joy. The ego and all obstacles have been overcome. Muslims are taught that this struggle is the highest and most difficult form of *jihad*.

There is a twelfth-century tale of a lovable, wise fool, Nasrudin, that speaks to this struggle. It also invites listeners to self-compas-sion as we stumble along trying to become better people. It tells us that we can learn from the missteps that we make so often. This is a teaching on patience, humility, and letting go. All are essential components to the attainment of happiness.

> "Oh, great sage, Nasrudin," said the eager student, "I must ask you a very important question, the answer to which we all seek: What is the secret to attaining happiness?"
> Nasrudin thought for a time, then responded, "The secret of hap-piness is good judgment."
> "Ah," said the student, "but how do we attain good judgment?"
> "From experience," answered Nasrudin.
> "Yes," said the student, "but how do we attain experience?"
> "Bad judgment."

JOY AND SUFFERING

It is uplifting, and at times challenging, to consider joy in our lives. We celebrate when it is present and fret when it is hidden. Although it is potentially with us always, we find it elusive. It takes many forms, from solitary bliss to celebratory jubilation, from euphoria to quiet contentment. But whenever we start to consider the many aspects of joy, its opposite comes to mind. Suffering is equally a part of our lives. We can anticipate both being present on a regular basis. In fact, joy and suffering can be seen as joined, one completing the other. As we age and pile up many years of life's teachings, we can see both forces flowing through us, alternating and at times present simultaneously.

At the height of our joy, we may become aware that it is a passing phenomenon. This can further elevate our experience as we treasure the moment deeply, or it can diminish it as we regret its impermanence. The response to this awareness is our choice. Likewise, when we are in grief or enduring any kind of suffering, we can also know this will pass. Nothing stays forever, although we may be changed by our pain. That change is also up to us. Will suffering close us down and create barriers of bitterness, cynicism, pessimism, and fear? Or will suffering open us to becoming more empathetic, wise, and compassionate people? It is through our deepening awareness of this pendulum of joy and suffering that we can witness them coursing through our days and choose our responses.

All these experiences are to be embraced and acknowledged as bridges to our world of belonging. As we share our joy and our suffering, we come to know our own humanity. It is at once extraordinary and singular, as well as universal and timeless. The particulars of our joy are known to us, but if we look deeply, they unite us to all those who have been uplifted in the same way. The depths of our sorrow feel isolating and beyond anyone else's comprehension. In fact, that very pain is the path to a true understanding of our brothers and sisters across all time and cultures. These opportunities to encounter our joy and suffering in awareness are ours to embrace. This may take courage, but it is the fullness of life that awaits us in these encounters with spirit.

NOURISHING JOY WITHIN

Care for our spirit is the foundation of our freedom and happiness. We see this as we reflect on the themes of forgiveness, simplicity, beauty, mindfulness, gratitude, nature, solitude, and silence. Here, let us add one powerful practice that has been helpful to so many over thousands of years.

The Four Immeasurable Minds of Buddhism are:

- Compassion
- Equanimity
- Lovingkindness
- Joy

They are an ancient Buddhist teaching and can be effectively used to care for all the thoughts and feelings that shape the nature of your days. They are called immeasurable because they are boundless and bring us to a place beyond ego, a place of freedom. Briefly, compassion (*karuna*) is our ability to understand another's suffering and to use that understanding to effectively be present and help. Equanimity (*upekkha*) is our ability to be at peace, no matter what is happening around us. This allows us to remain centered and stable in the midst of various disruptive occurrences, internal or external to us. Lovingkindness (*metta*) is our ability to hold ourselves and all those before us with an open heart. It is a generosity of spirit and hospitality of the self that welcomes all. Of course, this is easier for us with some people than others. That is the practice. No one is left out; no one is left behind. Joy in this case is particularly sympathetic joy (*mudita*). This is the ability to be genuinely happy for others' good fortune. It is to understand that what brings others happiness is related to our happiness also. In this understanding of life, what benefits one, benefits all. We are connected in interbeing, and we rejoice together.

You may find this teaching potent in shaping your worldview. For years, I have checked in with these four words daily by just asking myself:

- Where is my joy?
- Where is my equanimity?
- Where is my compassion?
- Where is my lovingkindness?

What has become apparent to me is the interconnection of these states of mind and heart. Feeding one supports them all. Difficulty with one strains them all. If you take your time with the four questions, you will find the source of any confusion or failure. You will also find the sources of your strength. They will help guide you back to your true self. Your contemplation will deepen with knowledge of the near and far enemies of the Four Immeasurable Minds.

The far enemies are the opposites of these desirable states of being. The far enemy of equanimity is anxiety, greed, or judgment. It occurs when we are not able to look at things in a balanced manner. The far enemy of compassion is cruelty. Certainly we know this when we see it. The far enemy of lovingkindness is ill-will or even hatred. These energies are also easy to identify. The far enemy of joy is envy, resentment, or jealousy. It is the failure to be truly happy for another.

The near enemies are harder to recognize in ourselves. We might even think we are doing well, being noble when we are missing the mark. The near enemy of equanimity is indifference. This is a hardening of the heart that is antithetical to spiritual life. We may feel we are protecting ourselves, but in fact, we are diminishing our own potential. The near enemy of compassion is pity. Pity is similar to empathy, but it comes from a position of superiority. Rather than extending ourselves as loving brothers or sisters, we offer ourselves from a position of greater strength. We need to aim for true empathy. The near enemy of lovingkindness is attachment. We may feel we love someone well and completely when what we are doing is harming them through our need to control and cling. The near enemy of joy is comparison or joy for others with identification. Comparison seems to be an instinct. We tend to measure ourselves against others in so many ways. In fact, someone else's good fortune does not diminish us. It is to be genuinely celebrated. Joy for others with identification can be quite subtle. This is when we are happy for someone else but also include ourselves. This insertion of the ego leads to "my" claims such as, "My son earned a scholarship," or "My team won last night." It wasn't primarily your action that led to these outcomes. You can take joy in these events without taking ownership.

These teachings on the Four Immeasurable Minds are buttresses for our spiritual joy. There are many ways to practice with thoughts and emotions. There are many ways to lift spirits in prayer, rituals, chants, and songs. But these simple words can go with you throughout life and attend to your well-being. They will guide you in days of suffering so you are able to touch joy. And in days of joy, they will lift you higher and higher.

NOURISHING JOY WITHOUT

There are many ways to enlarge our capacity for joy. Some are as simple as a chuckle. Pope John XXIII is an example of a person who delightfully employed a great sense of humor. When asked how many people worked in the Vatican, he quipped, "*About half of them!*" Then there was the time he was walking in Rome, and a woman remarked to a friend that he was fat. Overhearing, he stopped and went over to her and said, "*Madame, I trust you understand that the papal enclave is not exactly a beauty contest.*" And to a little boy named Angelo, he confided that Angelo was his name too, but they made him change it. It is that readiness to share a laugh that marked him as a person of joy. We can all celebrate this ability within us. Who and what makes us laugh? When was the last time we laughed heartily?

Laughter is good for us. Back in the 1960s, Norman Cousins chronicled the positive impact laughter had on his own experience of illness. Today, laughter yoga and laughter therapy have become popular modalities of healing. Research shows that laughter reduces stress and is conducive to psychological and physiological well-being. There are workshops and classes to join, but you can also simply watch a TV show or movie that makes you smile. Find a funny book to enjoy and then share it for double the pleasure. Surround yourself with friends who lift your spirits, and make time to see them often.

We also know that smiles are good for us, as well as for the folks we are smiling at. Thich Nhất Hanh tells us, "*Sometimes your joy is the source of your smile, but sometimes your smile can be the source of your joy.*" Science confirms his teaching. The muscles engaged in our smile communicate to our brain that all is well. When we smile, we release dopamine and serotonin, neurotransmitters that reduce stress and increase feelings of happiness. So even if we do not feel like smiling, if we try it, we can release these hormones that change our brain. And smiles are contagious, so turn your frown upside down and spread the joy!

There is a special place for the arts in the cultivation of joy. Music and dance have a direct impact on our moods. Just note how you feel when different types of music are played. And if you sing, how does that change you? You do not have to be a musician to enjoy singing in the shower or anywhere else. Dance and other forms of body movement alter how we experience ourselves in space. They empower us. Visual arts elevate our experience of life and connect us to people and events otherwise inaccessible. They are windows on the world and definitely lift us up.

It can be helpful to place reminders in your home and work environments to support your cultivation of happiness. Perhaps this will be photographs of loved ones or special places. It may be a favorite quote or piece of artwork. Wear a bracelet that has "joy" inscribed, or make the word your screensaver. Remind yourself to practice in these small ways to affect long-term change in your spirit.

Rebbe Nachman of Breslov told us in the eighteenth century, "*Finding joy is the hardest of all spiritual tasks. If the only way to make yourself happy is by doing something silly, do it.*" It can be hard to embrace our inner child and be silly. It can be hard for many of us to simply play. And yet, if we look to our childhoods, these talents were natural to us. We were born happy, and if we were lucky enough to be raised in a loving family, we had happy childhoods. As we got older, we began to respond more and more to the forces of our surrounding cultures. We may have started to see seriousness as a virtue and joy as frivolity. Spiritually, this completely misses the mark. We were born for joy. We need to keep reaching for the inner freedom it reflects. So, if you are happy learning to tango or want to go skydiving, do it. Do whatever is needed to discover joy, reclaim lost joys, and protect the joy you now embody. You will bless yourself and the world.

OBSTACLES TO JOY

As much as we might want to be happy, things get in the way. We often come into circumstances that steal our joy and threaten to leave us changed in a negative way. These obstacles to our joy take many forms, such as illness, death, divorce, ignorance, fractured relationships, job challenges, and loss of mobility. We can bristle when we are advised to buck up and move on, and rightly so. All suffering is legitimate. There is much pain to be endured in life. But it is important to look at our responses to these events, for there lies our spiritual opportunity.

The biggest obstacle to our joy is a lack of awareness. If we do not have ourselves centered in Spirit, we will be tossed about by life's struggles, like a rowboat in the ocean. We need to dedicate time daily to know who we are and to remain in alignment with our true selves. Difficult times bring anger, guilt, resentment, jealousy, pride, deceit, and so many unwholesome reactions. The trick is not to push them away but to hold them lovingly. Do not confuse these peace disrupters with the soul. We are not anger. We are not pride. We are not jealousy. These feelings course through us, but they do not define us, and we do not have to be hospitable to them.

We do need to acknowledge such experiences and bring them into the light of understanding. We need to recognize this part of our humanity and know that all facets of our lives are shared facets. It is easier to see this with aspects we deem positive. Everyone is able to love and show compassion. But everyone is also able to be deceitful, ignorant, and resentful. That is the human condition. As we acknowledge these enemies of our joy, we reduce their power over us and allow them to pass. As we become more skillful in monitoring our minds and hearts, we are able to reduce our experiences of negativity.

But as we cultivate self-awareness, let us remember that one of the gifts of a joy practice is to take ourselves less seriously. This is a powerful weapon against all of joy's enemies. Remember that angels fly because they hold themselves lightly. Let's all try to be a bit more like the angels.

THE PURSUIT OF JOY

There is a distinction to be made between the pursuit of joy and its practice. If we practice joy, we maintain our awareness of its presence and cultivate it in our lives. The pursuit of joy is a common distortion of such a practice. It is manifested by chasing after what we are told will bring us happiness. Our culture brings us these messages in both subtle and blatant ways. We might have been raised in a family that had high expectations of us. We learned that we were always falling short, never quite good enough. We certainly were raised in cultures that had ideas of what success looks like. If only we were richer, smarter, thinner, stronger, or wittier. If only we lived in a different neighborhood, in a grander house, had a nicer car, a bigger diamond. If only we were from a different culture, race, religion. Surely then we would be complete. We would be happy. There are many businesses, organizations, and people who jump right on to these feelings of emptiness to offer us their solutions. Often their enticing remedies come at quite a cost.

There is one pursuit I can recommend as a path to joy: the pursuit of service. Rabindranath Tagore shared, "*I slept and dreamt that life was joy. I awoke and saw that life was service. I acted, and behold, service was joy.*" The people who radiate inner joy have found a way to serve this world. They have been able to identify a lifestyle that resonates with their true selves. They live in harmony. And those who serve best also take care of themselves. This honoring of their own manifestation is part of their honoring Divine creation. They pursue their goals, small or large, as part of an orientation of reverence. Reverence is a wide-open doorway to joy. People of service touch joy with ease.

Too often, we pursue what is outside of us. That is a fundamental misunderstanding. Joy is not outside of us; it is within us. It is our natural state. We are born with the potential to manifest its power in our lives. Helen Keller, who certainly had reason to feel cheated by life, had this to say: "*Your success and happiness lie in you. Resolve to keep happy, and your joy and you shall form an invincible host against difficulties.*"

Here is the power in this practice. No one can take away your joy. You can be unaware of its sources within and around you. At times, you may feel defeated by life, and you may surrender your joy. But it is a choice, and you can choose to cultivate and claim joy. Julian of Norwich teaches us how. "*The fullness of joy is to behold God in everything.*" Joy awaits you always and everywhere.

QUESTIONS FOR REFLECTION

1. Remember what made you happy as a child. Can those same or similar resources be called on to nourish your joy now?
2. Who would you name as your patron saint of joy? What lessons has this person taught you? This person may be living or dead, personally known to you or not.
3. Think of some friends or family who make you laugh. Can you spend time with them? Tell them how much you appreciate their gifts of joy.

CREATIVE STRETCH

1. Think of a way you can bring joy to one person today. After you have done so, note how that impacts your own joy.
2. Take time out to explore the arts. Choose an option that will elevate your soul. It can be a visit to a museum, taking in a movie or a concert, or as simple as putting on some music as you go about your day.
3. Make a list of things, people, and places you would like to praise. Study the list, and then see if there is a way you can creatively express your feelings.
4. Spend a week smiling at everyone you meet. How does that feel?

The Joy Prayer

Divine Mystery,
You have placed us on the threshold of joy.
You have shown us how all of creation
pulses as one in this singing Universe.
Let us not turn away from your promise.
Let us not turn away from one another.
Bring us into the pure light of awareness.
Let us fall deeply in love with the beauty we move in.
Divine Mystery,
forever before us, beneath us, behind us, beside us, above us,
and yes, within us.
Let us claim the freedom we were born for
and let us radiate the joy we are
and send it forth in gratitude.

CHAPTER TEN

SIMPLICITY

"In character, in manner, in style, in all things,
the supreme excellence is simplicity."
—Henry Wadsworth Longfellow

On retreats, Thich Nhất Hanh used to tell a memorable story on simplicity. It is an ancient tale of a group of monks relaxing at lunch as they sat in a grove of trees with the Buddha. A frantic farmer came running up and asked them if they had seen his cows. He explained that he had lost all his sesame crops to a plague of locusts, and now his cows had run away. The monks told the farmer that they had not seen any cows and that he must look in another direction. The miserable farmer rushed off once again. As he departed, the Buddha looked at his monks and exclaimed, *"You lucky monks! You have no crops to worry about and no cows to chase after!"*

I keep a small statue of a cow on my bookshelves to remind me of this story. The question it asks is one worth visiting often. What are our cows? Certainly, they could be actual cows or a farm's crop, but they are also likely to be any of our possessions, our work, our projects, our relationships, our schedules, or perhaps even our spiritual pursuits. It is worth regularly spending some time reflecting on the complexity of our lives and seeing where things could be made simpler, and therefore lighter and in greater harmony with our true selves.

Simplicity is a virtue that has long been cherished in spiritual communities. The Quakers, Amish, and monastics in all religious traditions are living, visible witnesses to its value. This is one reason monasteries can be so restful to visit. As we pack, we take just a few things simple in design, meant only to be useful and comfortable. Perhaps we choose to take a journal, some special pens, a few books, and small personal treasures such as photos of loved ones and/or religious items. Most likely, we are asked to leave behind all electronics and to limit communication with the outside world. This stripping down of our lives is a bath of peace. The degree to which it nourishes us is an indication of our need for simplicity. We do not have to go to a monastery for this revitalization, but we do need to cultivate our awareness of simplicity's merits and the forces that obstruct it in our daily lives.

THE IMPORTANCE OF SIMPLICITY

Religious traditions employ ideas and practices that are worth our exploration. Why do people return to the same rituals, values, and concepts again and again? Nonviolence, peace, compassion, service, and many other themes recur across time and cultures. They are deserving of our assiduous consideration. Simplicity is prominent among them for many reasons. A simple lifestyle frees up our time, allowing us greater opportunity for spiritual practice. As our life is burdened less by material considerations and pursuits of the ego, we have an increased inclination to explore the mysteries of existence. The more we explore, the more we see the wisdom of leading a simpler lifestyle. Quakers believe that simplicity enhances our relationship with God, others, and ourselves. This strengthening leads to greater inner peace, serenity, wonder, concentration, and empowerment.

Simplicity is the ally of social justice. As Gandhi directed us, "*Live simply so that others may simply live.*" If we reflect on the inequities of this world, we can conclude that those of us able to read this work have been gifted with resources unavailable to much of the world's population. By doing with less and finding ways to redistribute goods and services, we make a contribution, however small, to righting fundamental wrongs. This puts us in greater harmony with ourselves and society.

Part of this world inequity stems from economic systems that promote endless consumerism. Recently I was looking at old photographs of my childhood home. My family was not wealthy, but we were certainly comfortable with both parents professionally employed. In old pictures, I see how simple our home was. Furnishings were purchased for value, including durability. What my mother called "good goods" were expected to last her lifetime and be handed down to the next generation. Antique stores flourished as people valued craftsmanship and the storied history of items.

Times have changed. We often comfort our restless selves with purchasing things we do not need and probably don't even want once the moment of acquisition has passed. We are sold a bill of goods that purchasing the right house, car, outfit, jewel, or techy gadget will somehow bring fulfillment. After an initial rush of pleasure, we are endlessly disappointed, and yet we repeat and repeat the action of buying again, buying more and buying thoughtlessly. This consumerism is destructive of our personal happiness, but we must remember that it also contributes to climate change, pollution, depletion of natural resources, and greater imbalance in the world. If we value the earth as our home and all its inhabitants as our brothers and sisters, we must do better.

In another demonstration of excess, Western culture is having a love affair with busyness. It is a feckless lover and one we would do well to dismiss. Somehow, we have come to believe that being overly engaged in our work, our personal commitments, our schedules, even our hobbies is indicative of an important life, a life of great value. In other cases, we can become busy in order to escape realities we do not want to face. We can work longer hours to avoid going back to an unhappy home. We can volunteer to boost our public image when our own loved ones need us. Often we do good works but simply too many. This is a kind of violence we perpetrate against ourselves. While we are compassionate to others, we are fundamentally unkind to ourselves. We need to take a step back and evaluate our lives when we see the signs of too much busyness. Are we stressed? Tired? Short-tempered? Then it is time to let go of some commitments and reorganize our time to support our well-being. This is basic to our inner peace.

MOVING TOWARD SIMPLICITY

It is easy to recognize the need for simplicity in our days but a challenge to implement it. As soon as things seem better, those familiar indicators of engulfing clutter arise. We can see the recurring need to clear our cupboards, to claim some solitude, and to let go of that one activity that no longer brings us satisfaction. So perhaps the first lesson of simplicity is that it is a matter of disciplined consciousness and continuing effort. It is not something accomplished and put aside. It is a practice that is available to us always and asks for our commitment.

How do we honor this commitment and implement the changes it calls us to make? As in all matters of consciousness, we need to make time to meditate and reflect. We need to know our true selves and all the resultant implications for our daily lives. No matter where we need to simplify, we must start by considering the situation carefully, in light of our values. The more regular this practice of solitary reflection is, the better. Take time each day to meditate, journal, walk mindfully in nature, or pray. There are many ways to stop and look deeply at our lives.

There may be times when you are thinking of simplification daily. It could become a burning issue by tripping over too many shoes or finding books and magazines piling up in every room. Perhaps you have cooking appliances that have been in their boxes for years or summer shorts with the tags still on long after summer has gone. At other times, you may only need to tweak some overscheduling of your workdays or a holiday season. When you pause and look at the stresses you are facing, you will know how much attention is needed and how to begin making change. As you seek to simplify your life and reap all the benefits that commitment offers, do not do so in a way that creates further pressure. Be careful to pace yourself and maintain your joy. We can look to our four-legged friends for advice on this. They often embody wisdom that we find hard to consistently claim ourselves. They live in the present, love unconditionally, and start each day anew with enthusiasm. So, in simplicity, as in many other matters, it is beneficial to follow the instructions inspired by my favorite pup.

Shake It All Off
Spirals of water arc off the pup's back
shaking all off without thought—
this natural fling of the unwanted.

And so too, let us send out a fast curve of debris,
useless habits, old hurts,
sticky desires, empty patterns of loving.

Release these detractors from your original self,
these distractors from the Universal Self.
Shake them off, and shake again.

Dark, reducing fears and sapping fantasies,
veils of opinions, judgments and worries.
Shake, shake, shake again!

Unhook the expectations.
Detach from praise and blame.
Smash the chains of pitiful bits of suffering.

Imitate the pup and send it all flying.
Roll in the grass and shout out a barking laugh.
Reclaim your own wondrous life!

MATERIAL CLUTTER

In the West, we are often burdened by our material possessions. Our homes cease to be restful havens. They have become overwhelming as they burst at the seams with our possessions. The more we have, the more we have to take care of. The overflow of items preoccupies us and takes our time and energy. We clean out one corner, and another waits for our attention. We spend our time finding new homes for valuable things and worrying about their relocation. It consumes so much of us.

This situation has given birth to a new industry. Real estate for storage has long been available for businesses. But now, there is a surge in personal storage facilities. They are booming, and 90 percent of them are in the US. As you travel the highways, you see them everywhere. In 2016, this industry of storage generated more than $32.7 billion in revenues. It may not be the glamourous side of real estate, but it sure is profitable! Why do we need them? Do we truly need them?

There are lifestyle considerations that have fed this growth. Here we see the impact of homelessness, death, divorce, downsizing, and dislocation. But my guess would be that consumerism is often the root cause. One used to leave a relationship with a packed car; now, one needs a van and a storage unit. How can we address this mess? After all, as someone wisely said, you can't put a U-Haul behind your hearse!

We do have choices about new purchases. We can increase our awareness of our susceptibility to advertising and peer influence. We make better decisions for ourselves when we know those susceptibilities and their power over us. When the option is available, we can decide to buy things that are not made with planned obsolescence built in. Often this requires that we pay more upfront, but it is a wise financial investment in the long run and contributes to the wellbeing of society and the earth. We can reduce the number of credit cards we hold and even decide not to use them. It does slow down most of us when we are required to put cash on the line. We can decide not to make any purchases for a period of time, for example, for a month or during a religious period. Perhaps for Lent, you would like to give up shopping beyond necessities. We can buy used goods. We can get creative and make what we need. We can exchange services and goods with others. There are many choices, and they become clear when we set the intention to consume less and consume more wisely.

We can also make strides in clearing out our living spaces and minds as we declutter our homes and offices. There are many great tips online and in popular books, but the most effective one for me is to simply take an item a day and dispose of it. I find a corner, and for a period of time ranging from a month to one hundred days, I put aside an item of clothing, a book, or whatever needs to leave. At the end of the time period, I donate everything. For me, it is easy and effective to do this. It can be hard to let go of some items, but I ask myself if I truly need it and/or treasure it. If not, then it is time to let the item pass into hands that do need it and/or will treasure it. Once that place is found, it is easy to release the possession.

There is a practice in Sweden called "Swedish death cleaning" that is growing in popularity. It involves the simplification of an aging or ill person's life in preparation for death. This may mean the selling of property, downsizing a home, distribution of excess material possessions, organizing paperwork, discussing plans with loved ones, and making any other possible contributions to a smooth transition from this life. I know several people who have done this without calling it "Swedish death cleaning." It makes eminent good sense. Do you really want your adult children reading through your journals when you have died? What about those years when you were nearly driven crazy by their antics? Some things are better left unshared. However, many people are so uncomfortable with their own mortality that they become paralyzed at the thought of making such changes. This is unfortunate because the more we have our lives in order, the more we have peace. We are all going to die. Let's not die and leave a mess behind.

MENTAL CLUTTER

All of us experience times of mental stress. We can be overloaded with input, especially in this age of rapidly changing technology. We can experience brain fog and memory lapses. We can be confused and distracted, and we can be worried to the point of panic. We can be "out of our minds." How do we cope? How do we simplify our mental activity so it becomes more centered and clear? There are a number of approaches. Some have been explored in other chapters, and they bear repeating here.

First, we need to seek some solitude and quiet. We may be inclined to do just the opposite to distract ourselves from our discomfort, but the wise first step is to just stop. When we create some internal space, we can then contemplate our own minds. We may decide that we want to talk to someone about our troubles or decisions that need to be made. But first, we need to look deeply inside ourselves. This requires solitude and silence. With your practices of prayer, meditation, and mindfulness, you will be able to move ahead.

Even deep in prayer or meditation, you may find your mind is running out of control. This is the nature of the mind. It likes to carry on, creating thoughts that can be helpful, distracting, amusing, frightening, or simply strange. Feelings also emerge and evoke more confusion. We simply observe, knowing this is the nature of our humanity, and gently bring ourselves back. We center ourselves again and again with compassion. This is a chance to practice non-judgment, which is also helpful for decluttering the mind.

Throughout our days, we spend a lot of time evaluating and judging everything around us. You probably are not even aware of these waterfalls of mental activity until you try to stop. Notice in a single day how often you make a judgment. It can start with the coffee, the weather, the tie your boss has on, the salad dressing, or an essay you read. It may be positive, amazingly nuanced, or harsh. It doesn't matter. It all takes your energy. So, this is a good place to make life simpler. Just note, "judging again," and let it go. Again and again.

The foundational practice of living in the present is a powerful practice for mental health. We stay in the moment we are experiencing with our full attention. If we need to think about the past, we do that with the same full attention. This is different than ruminating and replaying history. For the future, we need to plan and do so with all our concentration. This should not include the endless rehearsing of possible scenarios and the arousal of anxiety. We plan, and we let go. As much as possible, claim your life in the here and now.

The Buddhist practice of beginner's mind is also helpful to declutter the mind. When we enter beginner's mind, the first thing we do is empty it of all preconceived notions. There is a popular Zen story that explains this well. A wise teacher was often visited by people wishing to understand the teachings of Zen. One officious fellow came and asked to be told all the important principles of Zen to benefit his life. The master offered him tea, and when the visitor accepted, he started to pour. He continued pouring, and the tea flowed over the rim of the cup and onto the table. The visitor protested. "Don't you see the tea is spilling all over?" The master replied, "You are like this cup. Your mind is already overflowing, so you cannot receive the teachings."

In beginner's mind, we create an emptiness that is ready to receive reality as it is in this time and place, not with a lot of baseless preconceptions and expectations. This state of mind is the one that is most ready to learn and create. It is open to all possibilities and therefore most flexible and imaginative. Here we find new ideas and solutions more easily. It allows the mind to become the playground of the imagination.

When we are clear about who we are and what our purpose in life is, mental chatter calms down to some degree. There are fewer false starts and blind alleys. It is critical to work throughout our lives to grasp our inner compass and steer by it faithfully. Whether your ethical commitments are to the Ten Commandments of Judaism, the Yamas and Niyamas of Hinduism, the Mindfulness Trainings of Buddhism, the Sermon on the Mount of Christianity, or other teachings, let them be your guide. Life is simpler when we know who we are.

TIME AND CLUTTER

According to an old Irish saying, when God made time, he made a lot of it. Most of us do not feel like there is a lot of time. We look at the day, week, or month ahead and feel pressure from a lack of time. How will we get it all done? What about the important things we cannot get accomplished? What about the loved ones we are not seeing, writing to, or calling? How have we become such a time-stressed culture? And how can we declutter our schedules to allow more spaciousness?

Most of us will recall a time when we were young and lived in days that were long. The hours spread before us as unchartered territory to explore and relish. Summer days were especially unstructured and left open to our own creation. I can remember climbing trees to the top of our garage's roof and spending lazy days watching the natural world of our backyard. Squirrels were playmates. The changing leaves and visiting birds held my attention for hours. At times, I was joined by my friend, Martha, but I was content with my own company too. Other days were spent reading in a small attic window seat, a place no one else ventured. I don't think anyone knew where I was for many of those hours, and they would not have worried. Now, parents do worry, which results in heavily scheduled children, leaving few of their hours free for self-initiated play and explorations. This has a strong impact on everyone's experience of time, parent and child. There is evidence that we are actually a less-violent society today, but the concern for our youngsters' safety is real and pervasive. This impacts children's development in ways parents need to monitor and research needs to investigate further. Meanwhile, there must be a middle way where adults are reassured about safety, and children are encouraged to experience solitude and unstructured hours to fashion in their own way.

Technology has had an impact on our experience of time as well. We are all faced with choices about what screens to watch or interact with, and for how long. This is a major refashioning of our culture, and we are just beginning to learn to utilize technology well. Technology itself is a tool, a neutral implement that can be destructive or used for good. It is up to us to figure out how best to integrate technology into our lives. If we are spending a lot of time on our phones, we are losing that time for other pursuits. We are further crowding the hours of our days. On the other hand, we have learned in COVID times how critical virtual connecting can be to our well-being. It is our awareness and discretion that are needed here.

My mother bemoaned the coming of the automobile, just as I adjust to technology's explosion on the contemporary scene. She would fondly recall when visits would be arranged in the winter months between branches of the family. This was the slower time of year when such luxury was possible in rural areas. Letters would be exchanged, and dates decided on. Then they would pile into the horse-drawn carriage and be taken for a much-anticipated visit of several days. Shorter visits were not practical since so much was involved in making the arrangements. Time together was infrequent, but it was cherished when it happened. Conversations were long and deep, full of joy and shared sorrows. She longed for this time and, of course, I never knew it. My children will likewise never know my experience of time as we shift through the decades. Time calls on us to make the necessary adjustments to automation, technology, and other innovations, hard as this can be.

It is quite possible that we are also overcommitted. It is good to regularly take an inventory of our commitments and see if they are still appropriate for our lives. Many times, we just continue out of habit with clubs, volunteer activities, social organizations, and more. Are you still contributing to the group? Are you still benefiting from belonging? If not, consider letting go. The same review can be made of relationships. Are we hanging on to relationships that are no longer beneficial to both parties? Perhaps you do not need to see Uncle Reggie for lunch every week. Would once a month do just as well? If you feel that once a month would be plenty, Uncle Reggie probably feels the same. Meanwhile, as some time is freed up, you can look at people or activities you have been neglecting. Perhaps some of Uncle Reggie's time can be offered to a sick friend, or perhaps you can finally take that photography class you have been eyeing. An inventory of your commitments can lead you to actions that bring your days into greater balance. It is well worth the effort to take your calendar into your own hands and arrange your days wisely.

One of the largest areas of time stress is work. Here again, technology has had a significant impact. It used to be that one was truly released from work's concerns on days off and vacations. Now that everyone is on the internet, it is difficult to disconnect. Workplaces often expect employees to be available at all times for calls or meetings. This makes taking a break challenging, and it can feel like one's job would be imperiled if one did not answer a call, text, or email. Someone else would be willing to take your place after all; it is a competitive world. This creates a new level of work stress that is bound to have negative effects in the long run. Rest and renewal are requisites for good performance, and if they are not provided for, negative results will eventually show. It is in the interest of the workplace to provide true breaks for employees, but this awareness is slow to gain support. We are a culture that values work and productivity. Many do not yet understand that energizing breaks are critical to maintaining that productivity over time.

When we do have some free time, how do we fill it? Can we relax and "waste" time? Can we play? Do we feel the need to schedule something right away? Are we uncomfortable with unscheduled time and solitude? If so, it is good to take a deeper look at that restlessness. What is it that we are pushing away from our minds? Are we dealing with fears or anxiety? Are we depressed or disappointed? Take this gift of free time and open up its spiritual treasures. Do some reading on topics that will edify your situation. Pray and meditate more. If you do not want to be alone, spend more time with your spiritual community or join a new one. Meet with a spiritual director. Most of all, look within and make friends with yourself. Find your divine spark. You are a beautiful being with untold depths of longing, gems of offerings, and boundless love. Don't miss your own life. Release distractions and establish a practice of simplicity.

QUESTIONS FOR REFLECTION

1. When was the last time you experienced the sensation of endless hours? What were the circumstances? Can you offer yourself that experience again?
2. What and who occupies too much of your time? What steps can you take to loosen up these commitments?
3. What and who are neglected because you feel a lack of time? How can you take steps to accommodate these needs?
4. Have material possessions begun to burden you? Research places to donate your things so you can feel good about letting go. Break down the job to rooms or categories (books, photographs, clothes, etc.). Beginning is the hardest part.

CREATIVE STRETCH

1. Imagine you must leave your home in an hour, never to return. You have one suitcase for packing non-necessities. What would you choose to include? What does this tell you about your life?
2. Take a blank piece of paper and randomly record all the concerns that preoccupy you. Scatter them about in any way you wish. Include all your worries, unmet desires, anxieties, and longings. Do this over several days to be sure it is complete. When it is done, organize the items in lists.

   List 1—Things to begin.
   List 2—Things to get help with.
   List 3—Things to turn over to prayer.

   Once action is taken in any form, your mind clutter will be reduced.
3. Mark a day off on your calendar and tell no one. If anyone asks, you are booked. Indeed you are because this is a day to offer yourself. Begin the time with centering in prayer and/or meditation,

and then make an aspiration for the day that serves your true self. How you spend your time is entirely up to you. You may take a day trip or sleep on the sofa. Guilt for "wasted" time is banished, and joy is cultivated. Then, when your day is done, plan another one to savor and get it on your calendar.

A Simple Meditation

Repetition helps us calm and center. This simple meditation on the breath repeats a phrase on the in-breath and the out-breath. The words are grounding, and you may include anything on your mind as you settle in for your sit. For example, if you are upset by violence in the news you might say, "Breathing in, I am at peace. Breathing out, I am at peace." As you name your thoughts in this way, always returning to the breath, you declutter your mind.

Breathing in, I feel my breath.
Breathing out, I feel my breath.

Breathing in, I touch the earth,
Breathing out, I touch the earth.

Breathing in, I see the heavens.
Breathing out, I see the heavens.

Breathing in, I enter this moment.
Breathing out, I enter this moment.

Breathing in, I know it is fleeting.
Breathing out, I know it is fleeting.

Breathing in, I treasure this moment.
Breathing out, I treasure this moment.

Breathing in, I vow to love fully.
Breathing out, I vow to love fully.

Breathing in, I bow to all beings.
Breathing out, I bow to all beings.

Breathing in, I celebrate all creation.
Breathing out, I celebrate all creation.

Breathing in, I offer myself to life.
Breathing out, I offer myself to life.

Breathing in, I lift my heart in joy.
Breathing out, I lift my heart in joy.

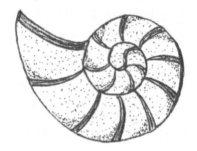

CHAPTER ELEVEN

BEAUTY

"Beauty is life when life unveils her holy face."
—*Kahlil Gibran*

B eauty is a challenge to define. It is elusive, and it is ever-present. It is fleeting, and it is eternal. It is blatant, and it is hidden beyond surfaces. Beauty is an objective moral value, and it is a subjective experience. It is up to each one of us to establish our own unique relationship with beauty. For as Gibran reminds us, beauty is an indication of the presence of the sacred. It can be employed as a pathway to Divine indwelling. Beauty has a number of aspects to reflect on that are elucidating.

BEAUTY IS SUBSTANTIVE

So much of the world is entranced with false beauty. The surface of the material world is lent considerable significance because of various cultural influences. It is not a new phenomenon. For centuries, a woman's bound feet were considered beautiful in China. All around the world, animals have been slaughtered so their furs could not only warm men and women but decorate them. Women's corsets created medical issues as well as hourglass figures. And so, the vagaries of vanities and whims have gone on and on. Today it takes many forms. We are barraged with sales pitches at every turn: TV, computers, phones, magazines and newspapers, billboards, movies, and even gas pumps blasting videos. Culture shapes our ideas of how life should be lived and what our lives should look like. Much of this influence we are not even aware of, but we are called to awaken.

Glitz and glamour are often mistaken for beauty in this commercial, celebrity-adoring climate. It takes some deliberate thought to step outside the everyday onslaught of input and evaluate it. Real beauty has substance. It is not shallow in meaning or deceptive in nature. Real beauty does not cover up; it reveals. We can easily be beguiled by a world created by advertising and media programming. But that is a path of endless dissatisfaction. There is always something newer, cleverer, and yes, more "beautiful."

We seek to boost our fragile egos with material goods, faddish activities, and expensive, unhealthy indulgences in food, drink, and exotic trips. None of these things are necessarily bad in themselves, but they are not the ground on which to build our identities. And, chasing these smoke dreams saps our energies—physical, financial, mental, and spiritual. So we need to be critical, wise consumers. What do we truly value? What is beauty to us? This calls us to deep looking and deep listening. It also calls us to practice with beauty so we develop a profound understanding of her and how she can guide our lives.

What makes a person beautiful? There are many answers to that question, but for me, the one that always works is kindness. Think of people you have known who are stunningly attractive but not able to extend themselves toward others. Then think of others known to you who are not glamorous, fashionable, or in any way trendsetters, but who are kind. Who would you say reflects beauty? For me, it is always found in the neighborhood of kindness. Could an unkind person ever be truly beautiful?

BEAUTY IS EVERYWHERE

There is an old Zen story about a nun who was traveling on a long journey. As the day was ending, she came to a small village and began looking for shelter for the night. She walked from house to house, but no one was willing or able to welcome her. Feeling desolate, she continued walking out of the town into the countryside. As dark descended, she saw a large, ancient tree with a broad trunk she could rest against. She made herself comfortable in its shelter and soon fell asleep, feeling lonely and disheartened. During the night, she awoke and looked up to see the most beautiful sight. The moon was enormous and sent down a warm light that fell upon the tree branches filled with blossoms. The nun gazed at the moon, the branches, and blossoms for a long time. Her spirit soared. The closed doors of the town had made way for this exquisite and beautiful encounter.

The story has several themes, including cultivating openness to the inherent beauty of reality. The nun knew to look up and consider her surroundings, even in her experience of rejection. We all need to cultivate this attitude of openness and expectation. The constancy of beauty awaits us.

It is within our power to create beautiful environments for ourselves and others. This does not have to mean large expenditures of money, but it does require clear intention and thoughtfulness. I once knew a young priest who moved into the inner-city housing projects of Troy, New York. With few resources, he created a serene and nurturing living space. He did it for himself, of course, but also to model living with dignity and beauty in adverse circumstances. His apartment was emptied, cleaned, painted, and then just sparsely furnished with live plants, good books, and simple pieces of furniture. It was a restful, warm, and charming home.

Many of us have much more to work with in designing our home and work environments. Often our problems lie in having too much. Clutter is not a friend of beauty. It does take time to create and maintain indoor and outdoor places that nourish our souls, but they are worth the investment. They reduce stress, inspire our creative life, and evoke joy. What is around us enters our senses and affects us in positive and negative ways. As you consider your spaces, think about noise levels as well as visual stimuli. Consider introducing music or chimes. Your home is your sanctuary. How you design it is your own expression of your inner vision. It is powerful in its impact, so let the impact be one of beauty.

Van Gogh said if you truly love nature, you will find beauty everywhere. Nature, in some form, is all around us. Even in inner cities, we find nature. We can explore the sky with its ever-changing face, its sunsets and sunrises. We can see the beauty of thunderstorms, soft rains, and sparkling snowflakes. Dandelions poke through the most unlikely places, and grass finds root in asphalt. If you or someone you know is housebound, plants, flowers, seashells, pinecones, and many other gifts of nature can be brought inside. They do not have to be many or extravagant to be life-giving. Bringing nature into any institutional environment is vital for all those living or working there. Nature transports beauty into these sterile worlds and builds connections to the Divine. Many people, unable to experience spirituality in any other way, can do so in the presence of nature. For us all, it is a homecoming. We are a part of the beauty of creation.

BEAUTY HEALS

Any kind of illness, whether physical, psychological, or spiritual, isolates us and is the breeding ground of anxiety and fear. Ultimately it can lead us to despair. Beauty is a potent antidote. Perhaps this is why flowers are so often brought to the sick. Flowers uplift us and remind us of our kinship with the natural world. Visual beauty, so helpful to the suffering, can come in many forms but include photographs of loved ones or places, artworks in various media, and objects of nature. Artwork created by friends and family, including children, can brighten any day. If there is even a spark of interest, art materials can be provided. An activity as simple as coloring can be quietly soothing and induce a meditative state. This helps a person relieve stress and heal.

During World War I, Carl Jung was the director of a prisoner of war camp in Switzerland. He started making mandalas spontaneously and found them restorative. Jung went on to use this art practice as a therapeutic tool in his work as a psychiatrist. In more recent times, art therapy has proved to be an effective mode of treatment for many conditions.

Sound healing is a growing field of research and practice. There are many recordings employing the right tones and rhythms to relax the body and mind. We know a state of relaxation promotes good health. There are also increasing numbers of sound healing events you can attend, and retreats in many traditions now include these experiences of deep relaxation.

Music has great potential for us all. Think of how moved you are by the music you love. It touches your soul in an immediate, powerful way. Music can induce a number of emotional reactions, so when our intention is to heal, it is important to select the right pieces. This is a good thing to do for yourself before illness strikes. Make a playlist; it is so highly personal. In his book, *Waking the Spirit*, Andrew Schulman shares his story of music and medicine. He demonstrates the potential of this field long practiced in music therapy but still far from totally understood.

Recently a beloved cousin of mine was in hospice preparing to die. Harpists came to soothe him and all those around him. This gift extended to hard-working staff as well as grieving visitors. This contribution of music is healing too, not to be confused with curing. We will all die, and transitioning with music and art around us will ease the way.

BEAUTY HOLDS IMPERFECTIONS

Beauty is a strong and large container. It holds flaws, mistakes, and a bit of ugliness with ease. Beauty transforms these bits and pieces if we give her the chance. In Japan, they have a term, *wabi-sabi*. *Wabi-sabi* celebrates the incomplete, the imperfect, and the transient, all as part of beauty. This aesthetic is rooted in Buddhism and its teachings on suffering and impermanence. It is an open and generous attitude of acceptance toward all that life brings. It values the worn, the simple, the useful, the natural, and the damaged. It is counter-cultural in a consumer-driven culture that strives for perfection through mass production, planned obsolescence, and artificially created needs and wants. *Wabi-sabi* teaches us to look deeply, cherish, restore, and repurpose. It is a wise way to move in today's world.

Leonard Cohen, the Jewish-Canadian poet, novelist, and singer-songwriter, offered another expression of this wisdom in his song "Anthem."

Ring the bells that still can ring.
Forget your perfect offering.
There is a crack in everything.
That's how the light gets in.

Indeed, there is a crack in everything, including our work, our material treasures, our vision, and our relationships with others, ourselves, and the Divine. When we can see our failings, our sufferings, and our death as light portals, they take on new possibilities. They become integrated into our lives in a more meaningful way as our teachers and our friends. All is embraced in beauty: all that has been turned away from, discarded, hidden, and neglected. Beauty leads us to wholeness.

A PRACTICE OF BEAUTY

Beauty comes to us unbidden, but we can also invite it into our days. However it arrives, we are given an opportunity to maximize its positive impact on our spirits. There are a few steps you can take to do this.

First, be mindful and recognize beauty. Let us not be so busy or distracted that we fail to see its many manifestations. This calls us to acknowledge the importance of beauty as a force for good. It deserves our attention and our cultivation. Many things tug at us and lead us down false and fruitless paths. Beauty is not one of them. Look for her with constancy.

Second, when beauty is spotted, take her into your heart and mind. Engage every appropriate sense and savor her. Pause. Look, listen, taste, feel, and/or smell with deliberation. Be present to this offering.

Third, receive beauty's gifts of nourishment. These may include expanded awareness, relaxation of body and mind, flights of imagination, empathy for other beings and the earth, and awe.

Fourth, be reverent. Acknowledge the profound impact of beauty. Know the cessation of ordinary time and enter the eternal present. Touch the Ground of Being.

Last of all, open your heart in gratitude for your practice of beauty, and when possible, share beauty with others.

QUESTIONS FOR REFLECTION

1. What is your earliest memory of seeing or hearing something beautiful?
2. When you were young, did your parents or another significant adult encourage your appreciation of beauty?
3. Name a place that is beautiful to you. Why? What are its qualities?
4. What works of art, in any form, move you? Name several.
5. Think of a person you consider beautiful. Why? What are her or his qualities?
6. Is there something/someone that you consider beautiful that other people don't?
7. How can you cultivate a practice of beauty?
8. What have you created that is beautiful?
9. In what ways are you beautiful? Name several.
10. How do beauty and spirituality interface in your life?

CREATIVE STRETCH

1. Visit a fine art museum and look at some artwork that is new to you. Is it beautiful? Why or why not? Select one piece that especially appeals to you. What qualities draw you? This is an enriching activity to share with a friend.
2. Attend a concert. As wonderful as recorded sound can be, there is a different connection available with live music. What are your experiences of sound? Note any physical reactions you might have.
3. What appears ugly to you? Practice deep looking and see if you have any change in your perceptions.
4. What sounds ugly to you? Practice deep listening and see if you have any change in your perceptions.
5. Try to perform an act of kindness each day. Each one is your beautiful creation.

A Meditation On Beauty

May I choose beauty today
Beauty to receive
Beauty to return

May I choose beauty today
Beauty in all my eyes rest upon
The sky above
The earth below
The faces before me

May I choose beauty today
Beauty in all I hear
The mourning dove's call
The fog horns on the river
The meditation hall's bell

May I choose beauty today
Beauty in all I taste
The sweetness of sugar
The freshness of cool water
The bitter pill

May I choose beauty today
Beauty in all I smell
The baking of cinnamon and spices
The roaring fire
The rose

May I choose beauty today
Beauty in all I feel
The warm weight of a quilt

The sweet pet's fur
The touch of a loved one

May I choose beauty today
Beauty to receive
Beauty to return

May my words be kind
May my thoughts be generous
May my heart be open
May my mind be clear
May my steps be careful
May my touch be gentle
May my eyes be compassionate
May my dreams be uplifting

May I choose beauty today
Beauty to receive
Beauty to return

CHAPTER TWELVE

A PRAYERFUL LIFE

"May you experience each day as a sacred gift
woven around the heart of wonder."
—John O'Donohue

Life is a mystery that holds much we will never understand. Our particular role is part of that mystery. Why was I born? What am I meant to do with my life? These existential questions can be difficult to answer, but they are rewarding to contemplate and work with over the years. Answers vary and change, but the beauty of the gift of life never does. We can enter that mystery and experience awe at our own manifestation and all of creation. This wonder is always available if we wish to tap into it. Sitting with it in meditation and prayer can lead to what is termed "absorption" in Buddhism or "mystical union" in Christianity.

Often when we pray, we are seeking change. We may wish to be relieved of a serious worry, an illness, or misunderstanding. We may long for love in our lives or world peace. Our list of desires is long, and we instinctively turn to higher powers. A crisis can bring us to prayer after years of silence. But there is another reason to pray. Prayer changes us. When we become prayerful, meditative people we increase our awareness of our circumstances and relationships. We come to know ourselves more deeply. We become less reactive and more reflective. Our true selves emerge, and we can live with well-considered intention. Ultimately, all our aspirations may be based in love. Our divine sparks are fanned. This alone is reason enough to lead a prayerful life.

TYPES OF PRAYER

"If the only prayer you ever say in your entire
life is thank you, it will be enough."
—Meister Eckhart

Prayers of petition are perhaps the most common form of prayer, but prayers of gratitude are essential. As Meister Eckhart tells us, they are enough. And if we can move from petition to gratitude in our hours of great need, we will be shifting from scarcity to abundance. This brings us perspective, an enlarged heart, and quiet, profound joy. All prayers and meditations carry great surges of energy. They are powerful and can be used to maximize support for the daily ins and outs of our lives. For example, if one is praying for a sick child, it would certainly be heart-centered to ask for recovery. But it would also be healing to recognize and express gratitude for all the days granted this young life so far.

Prayers can be formal and traditional, bringing with them strong connections to our history, our communities, and our ancestors. Prayers can be informal and simply spoken. These are moving in their immediacy and in the sacred unveiling of our souls. In addition to petition and gratitude, some other forms of prayer include praise of creation and the Creator, guided and sitting meditation, prayers for protection, mantras, gathas, chants, blessings, body prayers, and praying with scripture (*lectio divina*) and images (*visio divina*). The wide variety of meditation and prayer experiences allows us to incorporate a number of options during any particular day.

It is possible and desirable to pray in silence. Meditation, centering prayer, and other forms of spiritual practice do not employ words. They place us in a receptive mode of witnessing and listening. We can look at the beauty of the night sky and feel our hearts open in reverence. We can sit with a dying person and know Holy Presence. Silence is a threshold to the mystical. It is while listening to the Divine that we grow in wisdom and grace. Embrace the exploration of prayer beyond language.

When we do utilize language, our choices are important. Care should be taken to find prayers and meditations that are worded in ways that are spiritually supportive to our praying and to anyone who may be participating or listening. Language should be free of gender bias or any other form of discrimination that leads to separation. Care should especially be taken with children. We might relate to a phrase positively because of precious childhood memories, but if we are praying with youngsters, remember that we are also teaching, and our words should reflect a loving universe. For example, perhaps it is closer to Divine reality to say, "Creator, Redeemer, and Holy Spirit" than "Father, Son, and Holy Spirit." God is certainly beyond gender.

Do I have to address someone in prayer? What if I don't believe in God or have serious doubts? These questions come up in spiritual direction. Remember that prayer, in itself, will enrich your life. If God seems to be absent, know that your experience is a common one, even among the saints. It can help to find a way to address God that resonates with your spirit. Again, language is important. Here are just a few possibilities: God, Lamb of God, Allah, Morning Star, Higher Power, Yahweh, Abba, Father, Mother, Creator, Counselor, Love, Jesus, Hidden One, Emmanuel, Jehovah, Holy Spirit, Exalted One, Holy One, Divine, Beloved, Blessed One, Ground of Being, Friend, Manna, Source of All, Creator God, Prince of Peace, Physician, Redeemer, Shepard, Wisdom, All-knowing One, Teacher, Lord, Vanquisher, Almighty, Elohim, Protector, Beloved Mystery.

We can establish meaningful relationships with saints long deceased. The saints' examples of moral strength, courage, and lovingkindness can help us steer our own course. They can walk beside us through any difficulty.

Angels can act in the same manner. They play important roles in the theology of the Abrahamic religions. Many of us remember having strong relationships with our guardian angels when we were children. They were magical, spiritual friends who stood by our sides when we were frightened or lonely. Children seem to live closer to the invisible world. Often, as we matured, our guardian angels were discarded along with other aspects of childhood. For some, they remained present or were rediscovered in adulthood to offer guidance and solace.

Ancient Roman philosophers assigned archangels to the days of the week. There is an old tradition of uncertain source that assigns each of us an archangel depending on the weekday of our birth. If you don't know your day, it can easily be found online by submitting the date. It is interesting to learn about the attributes of each archangel, especially your own. Here are the archangels with their respective days:

Sunday: Michael
Monday: Gabriel
Tuesday: Raphael
Wednesday: Uriel
Thursday: Selaphiel
Friday: Raguel or Jegudiel
Saturday: Barachiel

You may find great comfort and inspiration in reaching out through prayer to those who have gone before us. There are levels of consciousness reached in our meditations that offer the possibility of connections we cannot fully understand. But the communion of the living and dead is a reality experienced by many in all religions and offers incalculable loving support. Love penetrates time and space at the invitation of our prayers.

SUPPORTING A PRAYERFUL LIFE

If you have ever lived in a monastery, you know how well supported a prayerful life can be. There are regular hours of prayer, work is a meditation, and a community of brothers and sisters surrounds and upholds you. It is harder to create a deeply prayerful life in the world outside monastery walls, but it certainly is done and done well by many. There are numerous supports that you can utilize to enrich your personal practice. Here are some options.

All space is sacred or has that potential, but you can make your home and work environments especially sacred to you. What this means will vary for us all, but it is helpful to choose a time and place where you will meditate and/or pray every day. This regularity helps establish a habit that stays with us wherever we are. You may wish to create an altar where you have inspiring images, candles, incense, and some presence of nature. You may wish to keep pictures of loved ones there, as well as people you are praying for at any particular time. Music and recorded meditations are helpful, as well as uplifting readings and your own journal. If you are a visual artist, you may wish to keep some art supplies in your prayer space. Other means of creative expression, such as musical instruments, may be kept close at hand. Reflect on what helps you connect to your true self and design a sacred space.

Other supports are found in mala beads, rosaries, holy water, bells, singing bowls, kneelers, and prayer rugs. Books of scripture, prayers, poetry, and other readings can anchor your sacred time. Some are organized as daily readings, which makes it simple. It is especially important to start the day with this pause for centering and direction. But then, you must go out into the world. How do you stay centered and on track?

There are many things to try. Gathas can be employed to make any task more thoughtful and, yes, prayerful. They are readily available in Buddhist materials but also easy to create yourself. Simply apply a few words of intention to whatever you are doing. Some examples are found in the next chapter. In your car, you can use music or recorded teachings to inspire you. On your desk at work, you can keep meaningful images and/or quotes. It is possible to set mindfulness bells on your computer so they remind you to pause and breathe at regular intervals. And remember, if possible, to engage in some type of body prayer, such as walking meditation or yoga.

There are many practices centered on food. As one becomes

more aware of the implications of our choices for the environment, animals, and our health, one can mindfully shop, being careful with each selection. You can then prepare your food in the same manner, saying a prayer or gatha to start. In monasteries, you will often find a small altar in the kitchen to dedicate that space. Perhaps at home, you have a kitchen windowsill or a corner where you could create an altar meaningful to you. Mine has a statue of St. Francis with a lamb and a bird that inspires me. I like to have a flower or plant next to it, along with a candle in winter. Francis' tradition honors animals, and I aspire to do the same through my food choices. When we sit down to eat, we can say grace and remember those less fortunate, especially those in need of nourishment. And when the dishes need to be done, we can wash them not as a chore, but as a mindfulness practice, slowly as if each one was a baby Buddha. When we are doing any chores, it can be calming to do them in this spirit.

Listening to music can change the atmosphere of any room almost instantly and help us maintain our concentration and peace. It is worth investing some time in identifying recordings that elevate your spirit. It may be classical music, modern sound healing recordings, or sacred music, such as chants and hymns. It may be all of those and more. Let the power of music infuse your days.

At the close of the day, there is an old practice of reviewing the last twenty-four hours called an examination of conscience. If you wish to do this, recognize what went wrong and look deeply, without judgment, to see the root causes. This will help you make positive changes over time. Be sure to also look at all that went well during your day and become aware of your accomplishments and inner goodness. Celebrate and build on your strengths. Keeping a gratitude journal is a wise way to conclude this practice and prepare for sleep.

You can also venture outside your daily routine and go on pilgrimage. This seeking out of sacred places can refresh your interior life. It might be a specific holy place, a holy well or mountain, or a location associated with a great saint. You can also design your own pilgrimage to landscapes that resonate with your soul. In the Celtic tradition, these thin places are where the holy is accessible, where the veil is thin, and you can touch heaven. Be creative in carving out these opportunities for yourself.

Spiritual communities can also offer you many benefits. They are dedicated to sharing prayer, meditation, and social connection through all life's joys and sorrows. They provide opportunities to attend workshops, classes, conferences, and retreats that will help you learn and grow. In community, you will find teachers and many kinds of interest groups to further your exploration of all things spiritual. More guidance on this is found in chapter three.

PAST, PRESENT, AND FUTURE

Nothing
in the world
is usual today.
This is
the first morning.

The author of this poem, Izumi Shikibu, lived in the late 900s in Japan. She is sending us this wisdom over many centuries, but the teaching remains relevant and rich. She is telling us that the ordinary is extraordinary. And she is telling us that this day is a new day, the first day. If we could only wake up with such a potent feeling of freshness and enthusiasm. In fact, we can. This attitude is a choice of disposition to live in the present. In Buddhist teaching, the emphasis on living life in the now is central. It is life-changing for those who embrace it and walk through life in the resulting mindfulness. Time is a human-made construct, and it can be strange. It can move slowly or extremely fast. It can be forgotten or carry all kinds of memories. It can be carefully measured or eclipse. When you reflect on eternity instead of the clock, your experience of time expands. It makes us aware of how we box ourselves in with schedules, deadlines, agendas, and calendars. We can be our own worst enemies when it comes to how we move through time.

Our tendency is to spend a lot of mental energy—and time! — thinking about the past and worrying about the future. This is not deliberate, thoughtful consideration, but roaming mental images, words, perceptions, and constructs that clutter our heads and prevent us from being truly present to our own lives and to those around us. It is fine to think of the past and evaluate our experiences. This helps us grow. It is enriching to enjoy a beautiful memory, perhaps of someone gone from us. This is a treasure. Further, it is necessary to plan and mold our futures. Doing so is our responsibility not just to ourselves but to others close to us. However, it is not helpful to get lost in our own musings, so we become agitated, depressed, anxious, fearful, tired, and stressed. Through a prayerful life, which brings us fully into consciousness, we can develop an awareness of our mental gymnastics. Our minds will always have a life of their own, but we can become keen observers of them and live with deliberation. Meditation is especially helpful to us in our quest to live in the present.

As you enter each day fully, allow yourself to dwell in wonder. Nourish that sense of awe and reverence that is central to your noble nature. Look within at your true self. Where are you? What needs your attention? How do you imagine your life going forward on this fine day? As you rest in stillness, experience the profound connection of all of life throughout the universe. Know that you are a part of it all, upheld by it all, and have within you a unique and irreplaceable Divine spark. Your creative contribution is yours alone to make. Say your prayers, meditate, and lift your heart in joy. Amen. May it be so!

QUESTIONS FOR REFLECTION

1. What are your early memories of prayer? Are these memories instructive to you now in any way?
2. What is your experience of the Sabbath? Include reflections on the past, what your current possibilities are, and thoughts about the future.
3. Is there anyone you feel you cannot pray for? How can this hardening of the heart be healed?

CREATIVE STRETCH

1. Write a prayer. Or, if you prefer, paint, draw, photograph, or knit a prayer. You get the idea.
2. *Vade mecum* is Latin for "go with me." Beginning in the 1600s, these little books were prepared as companions and guidebooks for those who carried them. Create one that inspires you. Utilize your own or others' writing and artwork. Give one as a gift.
3. Write a lorica, a prayer of protection for yourself or someone else. An example, A Lorica to Conquer Addictions, is found in the next chapter. Here is the formula.
- Make a list of your challenges or fears.
- Make a corresponding list of the opposite forces.
- List any special strengths or talents you have.
- List the angels, saints, deities, or elements of nature you wish to invoke for protection and blessing.

Starr's Prayer

Make of my life a prayer—
a prayer of praise, reverence, and wonder.
Let me move through each day mindfully—
mindful steps, mindful words, mindful thoughts.
Help me understand the power of lovingkindness
and show me how to infuse myself and others with its grace.
Let me not miss a moment of beauty's light—
illuminating, healing, and strengthening.
May all before me be recognized as holy—
each blade of grass, each being, each stepping stone.
May my soul fill with gratitude for all before me, big and small,
so I become a wellspring of generosity.
May I bow deeply at dawn and dusk
anticipating each threshold with courage and curiosity.
May I touch the source of joy that bubbles deep within my heart
and may I be released into perfect freedom.

CHAPTER THIRTEEN

PRAYERS AND MEDITATIONS

INTRODUCTION

T his final chapter is a further exploration of prayer and meditation. It includes messages from my heart to yours that revolve around universal themes. I hope it will encourage you to record your own prayers, to craft them with deliberation and authenticity. There are as many prayers as there are human beings. Believer or not, we all reach beyond ourselves into the unknown when we are in need or when we are touched in such a deep way that we are moved to reverence. These are moments to look at deeply and to cherish. They are an expression of our highest selves.

You may feel no need to create your own prayers. If you practice awareness, you will find that your prayers are often automatic. They may be without a single word. We can experience a deep connection with the Ground of All Being, perhaps the deepest, when in silence. This chapter encourages you to simply note and appreciate these moments of connection.

You may also enjoy traditional prayers. The prayers of our childhood can have a strong emotional pull for us. Perhaps we link them to our parents or other adults we greatly love. These feelings may grow with time, especially when we have lost those loved ones to death. It is possible to recognize that particular wording is out of date and even harmful to some, but not to us. It may be helpful to continue to enjoy these prayers. They serve a valuable purpose as they allow us to revisit early experiences of love and compassion.

But finding your own words for meditation and prayer can be extraordinarily powerful. They can help us gain clarity in our own thinking. They can help us communicate with others important to us in this time. And they can offer us comfort and healing. They let us rejoice, console, give thanks, praise, calm, and ask for help. Why not explore your own power of prayer and meditation further?

A Meditation On Time

Stepping back into time—
  touching memories of childhood,
  giggles, sobs,
  puddles, peanut butter,
  snow angels and swings.

Looking into the eyes of loved ones long gone—
  precious, present,
  holding and being held.

Gazing at roads not taken—
  wondering...
  smiling at roads not taken,
  turning away.

Gratitude welling from lessons learned—
  wisdom claimed,
  compassion embodied.

Stepping into the future—
  dreaming a host of possibilities,
  feasting on potential,
  floating in the lands of imagination.

Grounding in the present—
  dwelling in this moment, in all its richness,
  listening,
  smelling,
  touching,
  seeing.

Recognizing the miracle of this gift of a lifetime—
   reverent,
   humble,
   and grateful, deeply grateful.

A Lorica To Conquer Addictions

From the depths of isolating loneliness
I cry.
Barriers of failures, losses, disappointments
arise.
My soul is empty, a wandering ghost—
lost.

Let me know the courage of prayer.
Reaching out
to the Divine and all its expression of natural wonders.
Remind me of all the goodness I have seen
and the power of the ancestors who are my foundation.

Feed me with beauty.
Grant me insight.
Let all the paths before me be unobstructed.
May my choices be blessed.
May my inner strength manifest.

Calling all angels
to surround, protect, and guide me.
My guardian angel to walk beside me.
Be known unto me.
And may the great Archangel Michael
take up my cause.
May his sword remove all obstacles before me.
Clear my way to sanity.
Clear my way to peace.
Clear my way to freedom and joy.

Flower Meditation

Choose a flower that draws your attention. Do this intuitively, without a lot of thought. One stem is enough. Now set it up in a way that you can easily see it in meditation without moving your eyes or changing the position of your body. You are ready to begin.

Scan your body with your mind's eye. Make any adjustments needed to come to a quiet position of comfort and awareness.

Turn your attention to your breath. Let yourself relax into the breath for a few minutes.

Now look at your flower. What is its color? What is its shape? Follow the lines of the flower's form with your eyes.

Can you smell the flower? If so, what is your experience of the scent? Do any judgments arise? Let them go.

Let gratitude for this flower enter your being. Feel it swell your heart as you contemplate the beauty, strength, and healing powers of this small plant.

The flower does not come to you alone. It brings its roots and the rich soil that birthed it. It brings the sun and the rain that fed it.

Together we share the same home—Mother Earth.
Together we share the warmth and light of the sun.
Together we share the nourishment of the rain.

Now soften your gaze and relax into your breath as you breathe with the flower.

As you connect your breath to the flower, be aware that this part of creation is supporting you and your breath (pause).

Soften your gaze further or close your eyes.
Invite the flower's healing energy into your heart.
Feel the grace of its form.
Feel the glory of its color.
Feel the strength of its beauty.

Sit in silence with your flower (pause).

Now slowly come back to the presence of your flower. When you are ready, deepen your breath, lift your eyes, and come fully into the room.

Bow in gratitude to this small, precious being.

A Prayer Out of Grief

From this great darkness
I call to you, Lord.
My cry is a whimper.
The weight on my being crushes me
and faith flickers.

May your light shine on me.
Help me accept the pain of brokenness.
Strengthen my heart in gratitude
for this is the other side of love—
and love I have known.

Come Into the Thin Places:
A Meditation Inspired by the Celtic Tradition

Shed the day and
step beyond time into the thin places.

Stand at the shore where water
caresses the earth,
where the rhythm is undisturbed and
knows its own heartbeat.
Refresh yourself.

Wander on to the meeting of the waters
where streams converge—
a union of being so complete
two distinct pathways
become a new, singular reality.
Renew yourself.

Step into the sacred grove
and touch the blessings of
   the willow of the streams,
   the birch of beginnings,
   the ash of healing,
   the hazel of wisdom,
   the oak of endurance,
   the hawthorn of love.
Receive.

Dip into the waters of the sacred well
and feel a blossoming unfold within your heart.
Hear the ancient oracle of the well—
the priestess' truth calling you.
Recognize.

Lean on your pilgrim's blackthorn stick and
Gaze upon a standing stone.
Let its power, silence, and grace
seep into your every cell.
Re-member yourself.

Pause and rest in these thin places.
Pause and rest.
Re-member, recognize, receive, renew, refresh—
And rejoice!

A Prayer for Better Understanding

May my heart be open.
May it see beyond the outer manifestation of your being.
May it connect with the suffering you carry and find a way to lighten it.

Observing my judging mind arise, I smile.
Here it is again—and there it goes.
May the space between these thoughts grow larger.

May I come to recognize the limits of my perceptions.
May I realize the vastness of what is not shown to me,
and be grateful for all that is revealed.
May I always seek to deepen my understanding and compassion of
all beings.

Meditations On the Seasons

The following meditations are based on the four seasons. Of course, our experience of the seasons varies greatly with where we are located geographically, but these meditations are meant to acknowledge the passing of time, our connection to the rhythms of nature, and our impermanence. They also offer praise for the beauty around us and its Divine source.

The first two verses of each meditation are taken from the traditional Buddhist meditation on the breath as practiced in the community of Thich Nhất Hanh. Feel free to adapt the words to your own time and place and settle in to deepen your awareness and connection to all that is.

Meditation On Winter

Breathing in, I know I am breathing in.
Breathing out, I know I am breathing out.
In, out.

Breathing in, my breath goes deep.
Breathing out, my breath grows slow.
Deep, slow.

Breathing in, I enter stillness.
Breathing out, I calm.
Stillness, calm.

Aware of the season of winter,
I contemplate interbeing.
Winter, interbeing.

Aware of darkening days,
I invite deep rest.
Darkening days, deep rest.

Aware of birds migrating south,
I see empty perches.
Migrating birds, empty perches.

Aware of hibernating creatures,
I hear silence.
Hibernating creatures, silence.

Aware of fallen leaves,
I see space between tree branches.
Fallen leaves, space between tree branches.

Aware of flowers turned to compost,
I see sleeping gardens.
Flowers turned to compost, sleeping gardens.

Aware of ice on rivers,
I know fish swim in deep waters.
Ice on rivers, fish swimming.

Aware of birds leaving,
I see birds arriving.
Birds leaving, birds arriving.

Aware of bare tree branches,
I hear sap running.
Bare tree branches, sap running.

Aware of slumbering flowers,
I know seeds are preparing to burst forth.
Slumbering flowers, seeds preparing.

Aware of winter present,
I feel spring emerging in winter present.
Winter present, spring emerging.

Winter present, spring present.
Quiet rest of dark days,
entering light.

Meditation On Spring

Breathing in, I know I am breathing in.
Breathing out, I know I am breathing out.
In, out.

Breathing in, my breath goes deep.
Breathing out, my breath grows slow.
Deep, slow.

Breathing in, I enter stillness,
Breathing out, I calm.
Stillness, calm.

Aware of the season of spring,
I contemplate interbeing.
Spring, interbeing.

Aware of the coming of light,
I rejoice.
Coming of light, rejoicing.

As the days lengthen,
the sun warms.
Lengthening days, warming sun.

Patches of snow melt away.
The earth appears.
Snow melting, earth appearing.

Trees' bark unveils new color.
Birds return.
Bark unveiling, birds returning.

Snowdrops, Brigid's flower, appear.
Little bells calling us to worship.
Snowdrops appear, call to worship.

Crocus arrive in a blaze of color,
a balm to winter's white.
Crocus color, winter's white.

Flocks of winged ones fill the sky.
Birdsong lifts my heart.
Flocks of winged ones, birdsong.

Mud season has arrived.
Now in nature, always in me.
Mud season in nature, mud season in me.

Out of this primordial darkness,
comes endless beauty.
Out of darkness, beauty.

From inner darkness,
shines my true inheritance, my Divine spark.
Inner darkness, Divine spark.

Springtime is renewal.
Springtime is promise.
Renewal, promise.

All of creation infused with life,
manifesting Divine intention.
Infused with life, manifesting Divine intention.

Winter receding, spring arriving.
Winter receding, spring arriving.

Meditation On Summer

Breathing in, I know I am breathing in.
Breathing out, I know I am breathing out.
In, out.

Breathing in, my breath goes deep.
Breathing out, my breath grows slow.
Deep, slow.

Breathing in, I enter stillness.
Breathing out, I calm.
Stillness, calm.

Aware of the season of summer,
I contemplate interbeing.
Summer, interbeing.

Days have come into fullness,
full of light,
full of warmth.
Light, warmth.

Aware of the sun's blessings,
I bask in long days,
In generous, radiant days.
Long days, radiant days.

Aware of long days,
my energy surges forth,
my heart sings.
Surging energy, singing heart.

This is the season of water,
refreshing, cool water,
inspiring water.
Cool water, inspiring water.

Running streams, raging rivers, languid lakes—
All present their summer gifts.
Receive them joyfully.
Summer gifts, receiving joyfully.

The mighty ocean, source of all life,
mesmerizes and enchants.
Its shore calls again and again.
Mighty ocean, enchanting ocean.

Aware of the sounds of summer
Music is everywhere—
children playing, birds call, cicadas' song.
Sounds of summer, music everywhere.

Sudden storms arrive with drama—
thunderclaps, lightning strikes
and the descent of rain's refreshment.
Sudden storms, refreshing rains.

Aware of the energy of summer days,
I feel heat's invitation to rest.
Hammocks, beach blankets, and porches call.
Summer's energy, call to rest.

Aware of the gift of long days,
I can embrace play
and its nourishment of laughter.
Play, laughter.

Aware of the earth's greening
I see her glory in full bloom.
Greens of emerald, lime, forest, olive, and mint.
Earth's greening, full bloom.

Summer is the time of our greening too.
Come into the fullness of these days
with openness, gratitude, and joy.
Greening summer, gratitude, and joy.

Autumn will arrive bearing her own gifts.
The seasons cycle in a dance of reassuring rhythm.
Seasons cycle, reassuring.
Summer ending, autumn arriving.

Meditation On Fall

Breathing in, I know I am breathing in.
Breathing out, I know I am breathing out.
In, out.

Breathing in, my breath goes deep.
Breathing out, my breath grows slow.
Deep, slow.

Breathing in, I enter stillness.
Breathing out, I calm.
Stillness, calm.

Breathing in, I feel the freshness of fall.
Breathing out, I smile.
Fall's freshness, smile.

Leaves shine with color's glory,
red, gold, green, yellow.
Shining leaves, color's glory.

Leaves fall with ease and grace,
Offering themselves to the earth.
Leaves falling, offering themselves.

Streams ripple and bubble—
flowing around stones in their path.
Streams ripple, flow around.

Nuts fall, squirrels gather.
Preparations begin for winter.
Gathering nuts, preparing for winter.

Autumn's winds bring cool air,
Energizing, nourishing, cleansing.
Autumn's winds, cool air.

High in the sky birds migrate
seeking safety and warmer climes.
Birds migrate, seeking safety.

Days shorten cloaking us in darkness,
harbingers of winter to come.
Shortening days, winter coming.

Autumn fleeting, winter arriving.
Seasons turning in beauty.
Faithful autumn, faithful winter.
Faithful autumn, faithful winter.

A Prayer for A Dying Friend

May peace reside in the depths of your heart.
May you be comforted and free of pain.
May beauty surround you—
　　beauty in caring faces,
　　beauty in music,
　　beauty in a flower, a tree, a creature.

May you know your true value,
recalling all the good you blessed this earth with—
　　the kind words,
　　the gentle hands,
　　the welcoming smiles.

And because perfection is of the next realm, not ours,
may all missteps and mistakes be washed away by forgiveness—
　　forgiveness of others,
　　forgiveness from others,
　　forgiveness of self.

May you know moments of perfect clarity,
recognizing that you are intertwined with all that is,
that the sun shines within you
and the moon watches over you.

May you feel prepared to cross this threshold
and may you be lifted in joy to perfect freedom.

A Prayer for A Newborn Child

Welcome to this time and place
Precious One.
You arrive as a Divine messenger to us all,
perfect in every way.

May we be worthy of your presence.
May we be wise in our care.
May we be gentle always, and
may we cherish your heaven-sent gifts.

May you know great happiness.
May you grow in wisdom and grace.
May you delight in your own spirit.
May you explore the wonders of this world.

When sorrow comes, and come it will,
may you turn to face it with a steady gaze.
May you contemplate its depths
and may you transform it into compassion.

And when your days come to an end, and end they will,
may you know the joy of a life well-lived.
May your heart be fully satisfied
and may you dwell eternally in God.

A Prayer For Healing

Dear Lord, help me ward off all demons—
  Demons of seductive obsessions,
  Demons of addling addictions,
  Demons of pitiful despair.

Dear Lord, return me to wholeness.
  Heal my torments and my trials.
  Heal my heart and my soul.
  Heal the still hidden fractures of my being.

Return me, dear Lord, to the strength of joy.
Return me to the glory of beauty.
Return me to the light of love.

Amen.

For Sanctuary

Across millennia humanity has sought sanctuary.
We seek safety, refuge, contemplation, and prayer.
We seek community and ritual, solitude and silence.
We seek the still point of a manic world.

So sacred places appeared in groves, mountaintops,
And all the thin places.
Women and men created stone circles, sweat lodges, stupas,
holy wells, temples, mosques, chapels, churches, and shrines.

In these havens from life's storms,
all seekers find rest and renewal.

The light of Divine inspiration shines through nature and scripture.
The veil between worlds is lifted by music, chant, candlelight, sage,
peace pipes, bells, and all manner of sacred art.
Sacramental invitations.

Here we find the portals to our ancestors
and here they teach us, voices over the centuries.
Their spirits are felt in these, their havens.
We pray in the shelter of their love.

Let us set our hands and hearts to protecting and strengthening
every form of sanctuary for the generations to come.
Let all sacred arts be honored and flourish.
In this complex world, let all souls find the shelter of belonging.

And let all peoples grow in loving compassion
in the sanctuaries of their own hearts.
Sanctus, sanctus, sanctus.

Meditation On Old Age

Coming into stillness,
we contemplate old age.
Guarding our judging minds,
we look deeply at reality.

Our bodies talk to us often,
increasing their messages each year.
Their long, faithful service is signaled in
creaks, discomforts, and pains.

Our senses are shifting too,
Withdrawing in their own ways—
lost words, blurry sights,
declining smells and tastes.

Memories fade or become confused.
(Sometimes that serves us well.)
But staying present each moment
is the ultimate cure for a wandering mind.

At times we seem invisible or
we are greeted with new attitudes—
patronizing, obsequious, impatient—
all sparked by our outer shells.

Opening our hearts,
we hold the bearers of these judgments in compassion.
We recall that we were once young and rash.
May time bring them into understanding.

We rejoice in our bodies
still serving us today.

As some faculties change, others strengthen.
Consciousness expands.

Our sense of humor has become critical
to our well-being.
Laughing at life's many surprises
saves the day, daily.

Life has taught us
what is important, and what isn't,
what requires our attention, and what doesn't
and what is worthy of our devotion.

A well of strength is within us now
fed by decades of love, losses, and beauty.
It is the unexpected revelation—
the way made clear.

As our minds turn inward,
we prepare for our transition.
So many we love have gone before us.
We trust in life's rhythms, a holy plan, and grace. (Bell 3x)

Gathas

In the Buddhist tradition, there are short prayers to help practitioners stay in the present moment. The words are said to bring one's attention to a particular time or activity and to set an intention. Gathas are short, easily learned or composed, and may be adjusted to meet any changing situation. It is great to write your own so that the words call to your heart and mind. Here are a few of mine to get you started.

On Waking Up
Waking up behind closed eyes,
I stretch.
Entering the day on wings of gratitude,
I smile.

Putting on My Coat
As I put on this coat,
peace surrounds me.
Let peace carry me forth,
wherever I go.

Turning on the Computer
This cyber world is full of wonders and information.
Logging on, may I be clear in my intentions.
May I not drift into distractions.
May I not let a minute become an hour.

Going for a Walk
As I step out into the day,
let me center myself.
Let my eyes and ears be open
to receive the beauty that surrounds me.

Starting the Car
May the bodhisattvas and angels surround me
as I drive.
May everyone on the roads be safe
and arrive at their destinations in peace.

To My Readers

Thank you for reading *Divine Sparks*. I am deeply grateful to each and every one of you, and I hope that, in these pages, you have found new insights and inspiration for your spiritual practice.

What does an author stand to gain by asking for reader feedback? A lot. In fact, it is so important in today's publishing world that they've coined a catchy name for it. It's called "social proof." And in this age of social media sharing, without social proof, an author may as well be invisible.

So if you've enjoyed *Divine Sparks: Interfaith Wisdom for a Postmodern World*, please consider giving it some visibility by reviewing it on Amazon or Goodreads. A review doesn't have to be a long critical essay, just a few words expressing your thoughts, which could help potential readers decide whether they would enjoy it, too.

You can also connect with me online.

Facebook: https://www.facebook.com/Starr-Regan-DiCiurcio -Author-100390259026783
Instagram: @starrdiciurcio
Website: www.StarrRegan.com

My prayers go with you on your spiritual journey. May you be blessed!

Starr

CPSIA information can be obtained
at www.ICGtesting.com
Printed in the USA
LVHW101018171222
735431LV00005B/423